THE PODCASTERS COOKBOOK

A Step by Step Guide to Producing Professional Podcasts

What you need to know to become a successful Podcaster

STEVE JOHANN

Producer, Creator & Communicator

Attention Reader

After reading this book, you may decide it's too complicated or time consuming to produce a professional podcast. Don't let that stop you. I'm here to help you with all the heavy lifting through my stand alone production studio, should you wish to avail yourself of my services. As a reader, you're entitled to a free 15 minute phone call to go over your needs and see if it makes sense for me to help you. To schedule your free phone call, just email me at steve@stevejohann.com and I'll follow up accordingly. You can also visit my website www.stevejohann.com for more information.

Contents

Introduction
Producing a Podcast is as easy as Baking a Cake, Well Sort of

If you have never baked a cake before, the idea of making one from scratch might seem to be a bit daunting. But with the right cookbook and ingredients in hand your fears and trepidations soon turn to anticipation of eating the finished product of your labors in the kitchen.

Creating a podcast is much the same albeit a much more complicated process. But once you have the instructions in your hands and the right equipment and a couple test shows under your belt you won't be as intimidated as you were when you first set out to create your first podcast.

When setting out to bake a cake you have to first purchase the tools as in mixer, mixing bowl, spatula, measuring cups, a working oven and a baking pan along with a number of other items. Since you are going to make it from scratch you'll also need the proper ingredients and you will certainly need a Cook Book which explains in detail the exact ingredients, the exact amount of those ingredient and the correct order to place ingredients into the mixing bowl along with the amount of time needed to cook and the right temperature to bake it at.

Let's be honest, not very many people bake cakes from scratch today. Instead they buy a box of premixed cake mix. But it wasn't always this way and for the true bakers among us we prefer to bake from scratch. This way we can make sure to use only the freshest and most tasty ingredients. That's why cookbooks were invented so anyone with a bit of sense could follow the directions and come out looking like a chef. Cookbooks explain how to bake almost anything using detailed instructions and ingredient lists.

Now that you have this picture in mind, you can think of this book as your podcast cookbook that guides you in producing a professional podcast.

Why This Book Was Written

1. To help demystify the world of podcasting and keep you from spending a ton of time and money

Unfortunately there are countless people out there who are willing to take your money but give you very little in exchange. It's all about selling you "The Dream" but not giving you the complete story as to weather you will make money or not.

I hate rip offs and the internet is full of them. This book is designed to help you from being ripped off by podcast gurus selling you empty hopes and high priced mentoring programs.

2. To help you make an educated decision before you go into podcasting

Podcasting is a wonderful use of your time and money if you know why you are podcasting. It can also be a huge waste of time and money pit if you aren't aware of the real costs associated with podcasting. I wish to give you a heads up to what really goes into podcasting so you'll go into it with your eyes wide open, not shut.

3. To educate you enough so you can move forward on your own should you chose to

There is a lot to podcasting from the technical side to the psychological side. This book covers both. It will help you understand what goes into the whole process of producing a podcast from beginning to end. It will also help you produce a show that attracts an audience and future sponsors and clients.

4. To introduce myself and my philosophy to podcasting

I love helping people and this book is my way of helping you. I have been helping individuals and corporations grow their business for the past 25 years as the owner of Sound Image Solutions

Marketing Agency, my writings and podcasting and 1 to 1 coaching. This book is an extension of this.

5. To give you an overview of both the podcasting and broadcasting world, so you can apply it to creating successful podcasts

I am of the belief the more knowledge you have related to the world of media the better equipped you will be in creating successful podcasts and possibly other media properties. By learning what works in the greater Broadcast world you can emulate it with your podcast.

1

About Me
A Brief History of My Life as a Podcaster

I am an award winning 8 year veteran podcaster with experience in traditional broadcasting and online broadcasting. I started podcasting in 2007 and haven't looked back. I am the creator/producer/engineer and co-host of a weekly show called The Hog Radio Show Motorcycle Podcast which began airing (podcasting) November 17th, 2007.

The Hog Radio Show has over 450 episodes and is still going strong. In over 8 years of producing the show, I've had the pleasure of booking and interviewing well over 325 guests some well known others not so well know. It has opened doors for me to attend various industry shows and functions as a person of the Media. It has also afforded me the ability to create some really cool friendships that would never have been formed had I not begun this show back in 2007. I am respected for what I do by industry professionals and custom Bike builders alike.

The show continues to open new doors for me as an individual and as a business owner. I have also formed a strong bond with my long time host Walt Fletcher who has also benefited greatly by his association to the show.

We launched the show from the third bedroom of my home which doubled as my home office. I eventually moved into an office space not far from my home. This move, allowed me to be able to bring in more guests to the studio than the former 3rd bedroom.

Over the years we've been able to bring into the studio some really cool guests but most of the time we do our interviews via phone.

The farthest interview we've done was with a guest who lived in Spain. We used Skype and connected with him via his Skype app on his smart phone while he sat at a bar in a casino. His time was 4AM to 5AM in the morning, while ours was 7PM to 8PM.

One of the funniest incidents we've had on the show was when one of our guests was talking to us via cell phone while at a restaurant. While we were interviewing him unbeknownst to us, he had decided to step into a bathroom stall at the café to get away from all the noise. This was working well for him, until we heard the distinct sound of a flushing toilet. We had to ask him what's up with that. He then came clean and explained where he was. Suffice it to say, the occasional background noise was hilarious.

On the flip side I've had my share of challenges such as having to start all over again after my online provider yanked the chain on providing podcast services which caused me to lose nearly 7 years of connectivity. I had to basically start all over again.

When I'm not tied up with the show, I help people launch their own media properties and grow their businesses through marketing tactics and media properties. In addition I love to write which is why you are now reading this book. I state this because there are countless online marketers who hire an individual from Indian or Philippines and pay them 40 dollars to create a hack job e-book for them then place their name on it and sell it through their online portals and Amazon. NOT ME! I prefer to write my own books.

I'm a writer and teacher at heart and love to help companies and individuals grow their enterprises through my services as a marketer, consultant and podcast production advisor. With 8 plus years of broadcasting and podcasting along with 25 years as a marketer, I have a complete understanding of the potentialities and pitfalls of podcasting.

I Don't' Like Rip offs!

I hate to see people ripped off by con artists selling services aimed at well meaning but ignorant individuals who hear about the power of podcasting and want to start podcasting as a means to bolster their brand or name. Keep in mind, the term ignorant is not a derisive term, just an honest look at people who don't know about something they wish to go into. I am ignorant of many things but that doesn't mean I am stupid, so don't take my words as a statement of your I.Q.

Con Artists have owned the late night airwaves of Television and weekend radio stations for decades. These types will fill you up with how easy it is to make a killing, through house flipping, stock trading, and dozens of other get rich schemes and will sell you their high priced course which ends up not being used by those who purchase it or is not enough info so you must buy into their special inner circle group which of course costs even more money.

As a matter of fact these slick marketers were the very first to pioneer long form infomercials designed to sell you on the dream verses the reality. They are masters of harnessing the blind hope of individuals seeking an escape from their dead end job and channeling it into the purchase of their products and services. I call these types dream sellers who sell you on the dream verses reality.

Today these very same types have harnessed the internet to sell their info products. They have mastered the art of the Long Form Sales Landing Page or the online webinars designed to give you all the reasons why you should buy their products or services. They also use their podcasts as platforms to sell you on their services.

These types are masters of wetting your appetite to get you to want more. They understand the power of selling hope rather than a real business. They understand how to manipulate your need for significance and transform it into purchasing their products and services.

These hucksters have tapped the Get Rich Quick Now Mentality that has made casino owner's billionaires while making their marks bankrupt. These marketers know there are thousands of people who will pay them for the chance at hitting the jack pot.

These masters of illusion have made hundreds of thousands even millions through their courses, books, seminars, reports and so many other info related products. They have muddied the waters of Honest Service Providers.

I have fallen a number of times over the years for these very same illusionist tactics. I've bought their courses and books. I, like many a sailor, was lured to the rocks by the sirens call of riches. In the end, I ended up being looted of my hard earned money. I know what it means to be hoodwinked into thinking if I purchase their book or products I will have the keys to the kingdom.

I no longer listen to these hucksters instead I even call them out. Now I use my voice to warn people and I use my expertise to help people move forward without being ripped off in the process. My goal for you is to operate from a place of knowledge, not ignorance.

If you're like me and you're tired of being taken advantage of, then, I think after reading this book you'll agree with me, that it was worth your time and money. Consider this book, my way of sharing with you some of the things I've learned the past 10 years.

2

Podcasting a New Media Platform

One of the coolest aspects of podcasting is how it opens doors to many other opportunities. If you follow what TV and Radio has done to create platforms for individuals and apply it to podcasting you will be able to emulate what has been achieved by various individuals at a lot less cost to you.

In this book I draw a lot of parallels between Traditional Media (Radio/TV) and New Media (Podcast/YouTube) to give you a solid foundation by which you can create a quality show. What works for traditional media also works for podcasting.

The only thing that has changed is the way in which you can reach your audience and the way you produce the show. What used to be relegated to the radio waves and a radio station has now been opened up to anyone with internet access and a home studio.

Podcasting and You Tube have opened up the doors to the world of media for all peoples and as an outcome it has birthed many an entrepreneur and entertainer. There are wealthy people who began their career on You Tube or through Podcasting. There are also thousands of people who will never get rich but still have fun sharing their thoughts.

The internet and technology has provided an equal playing field to anyone who has a creative bone in their body. It has opened doors to writers, screenwriters, movie makers, DJ's, Talk Show Hosts, reporters and marketers.

I am a firm believer that you should learn from what has worked in the past and emulate successful people and formats to attract an audience or make money. This is why I draw a lot from the world of Traditional Media especially Radio because it's the original audio content delivery system.

Podcasting, like TV and Radio, is an exceptional way to get yourself into circulation as it provides you a mechanism in which you can reach people and build an expert position you would never come into contact with otherwise.

Keep in mind the world of New Media which includes You Tube and Podcasting, there is probably 20,000 people or more sharing their passions with their audiences. I would also go as far as to say 80% of all these personalities or organizations are not making money directly from their show. Some use it to as a platform to sell their services and products from. Others do it for the pure joy of having people listen or watch them.

Much like people who are passionate about golf and have no problem spending thousands of dollars and hundreds of hours playing golf, there are as many of us who go into podcasting for the same reason. Podcasting is an excellent creative outlet for many of us.

Just as there are a relatively small number of golfers who make a living at playing golf there are also a small number of podcasters who make a living podcasting. But that doesn't stop the rest of us from enjoying the very same activity.

For those who do wish to profit from podcasting you can and this book and my services are dedicated to helping you do just that. I've found those who do make money from podcasting or You Tube are companies and individuals who understand the medium for what it is and have learned to leverage it as part of an overall marketing plan not as their sole marketing avenue.

A Brief History of Podcasting

According to www.internationalpodcastday.com the inventors of the podcast are Adam Curry and Dave Winer who launched the podcast platform in 2004. The term Podcast was coined by Ben

Hammersley January 2004 in an article posted in the Guardian News Paper.

In January 2013 Apple announced it had 1 billion podcast subscribers! Wow now that's a lot of people listing to podcasts! Who would think such a number of people around the world would be tuning in to listen to their favorite shows and discovering new shows in such a short time.

As you can see within 12 short years huge inroads have taken place within this totally online world of podcasting. Celebrities have been born on the podcast platform, radio show hosts have increased their fan base using podcasting and companies have been able to take advantage of this platform to better serve their customers and win new customers.

No matter where you are in the world of podcasting whether you are a beginner, long term podcaster or someone kicking the tires, all it takes is a desire, a few dollars and a willingness to learn and you too can transform your enthusiasm into a cool weekly show all of your own.

Keep in mind you can listen to podcasts on your Android cell phone thanks to Stitcher and a number of other apps and you can listen to them on your iPhones through the iTunes application.

The next ten years will see an even bigger increase in daily listeners to podcasts as well as more mainstream content being diverted to the podcast format. The question for you is this, after you read this book will you jump on the podcast train? Hopefully you will because now is as a good time as ever to climb aboard the podcast train.

Podcasting Your Ticket to Near Celebrity Status

As a podcaster you probably won't be able to quit your day job any time soon but you'll sure make a lot of friends and new business contacts. If you're wise you might just make some money along the way to.

The biggest thing you have to keep in mind is podcasting is narrow casting. In all likelihood you won't reach millions of people (there are a few who do) instead you're more likely to reach thousands. Most hosts would be happy to have several thousand at any given time listening to their show. Unlike radio, which is just a click away on your radio and has a hundred year track record, podcasting is new. To listen to a podcast is a multiple step process that keeps many people from tuning in on a regular basis. This multi step process makes it easy for listeners "forget" to tune you in.

People are creatures of habit and often find it easier to not go online then go online to listen to media but this is changing, thanks to Phone Apps that allow people to listen to their favorite shows anytime they wish. The demographic for media consumption is changing and most consumers under 35 are huge consumers of online media. This means there is a huge audience to tap into, who listen to their music and audio content through their smart phones, tablets and computers.

Podcasting affords you the ability to create for yourself cult status or expert status and to become a sought after celebrity in small knit circles of avid fans. If you prove you're worth listening to, you may become the next expert in your niche industry.

Just watch any cable "news" television show for any length of time and you will note how many times these shows trot out their favorite experts to share their knowledge about the latest crises being featured. These so called experts are called upon to give their point of view on these subjects.

Have you ever wondered where these experts come from? In many cases it was through some affiliation between the producer and the expert and here is where podcasting can become interesting. Let me explain how this might work for you.

The expert is first approached by the TV Show producer to come on and share their thoughts, which they do. Once these personalities come on and do a great job they are put on a short list should the show producer need an expert in this given field. Next time the same issue arises, guess who they call? Yep, the same person is asked to return when it comes to delving into the same topic. Soon these experts become regulars on these shows and after a while they gain nationwide notoriety and are able to leverage these media appearances and use them to further their careers.

Bill O Riley started out as nothing more than an on the street news reporter for a New York TV station. Dr Phil got his start by first appearing on the Opera Show. Opera liked him so much she brought him back on again and again until the network saw how well he did for ratings they created a show for him. The very same thing happened to Dr Oz, Jim Cramer and many other personalities even the likes of Jay Leno got his start appearing as a comedian on the Johnny Carson show a number of times. When it came to filling in for Johnny while he was on vacation they called upon Jay. He did a better job than other personalities so when Johnny retired Jay landed the job.

You can do the same thing with your podcast platform to help yourself get noticed. You can leverage your status as a means of getting booked on other shows. This will eventually lead to being invited to speak at various events which then open doors for more things. You can also reverse this process by inviting people you admire onto your show to be interviewed with whom you wish to do business with in the future.

As much as everyone wants to get advertisers on board from the get go most sponsors won't come on until you have a sizable fan base. By starting a podcast you automatically elevate your name above your competitors who don't have a show.

How Podcasting is Currently Being Used

The following is a list of ways podcasting is currently being used. I say current because I suspect there will be other ways podcasting will be used in the future.

1) As an extension of a media property that already exists: Magazine, Blog, Online publication, TV show, Radio Show.

2) As a marketing tool: An example is Bass Pro Shop produces a podcast related to outdoor activities which lets the company not only talk about the passion of outdoor life but also promote the store and products being sold in it.

3) As a way to build expert or celebrity status for your self, much like a Radio or TV Show, Blog, Book or Video production does. People will assume by virtue of your presence as a podcaster that you are a professional who knows what they are talking about. That is unless you don't sound professional then you will lose respect.

4) As an infomercial. Podcasting is an exceptional way to market yourself and your company. It's an easy way to promote your products and services as in a short form or long form infomercial, similar to marketing but slightly different.

5) As a lead generation magnet. By placing the podcast on your website you will drive people to your website on a scheduled basis. By having it up on ITunes it will be a beacon to bring people to your website, etc.

6) Personal platform to fulfill a dream of becoming the next Rush Limbaugh, Garrison Keeler or (put your favorite talk show host here). Yep, it's true; many of us have dreams of being radio show hosts but can't break into traditional radio. Podcasting provides a pathway of hosting your own weekly show without the expenses that accompany traditional radio. Additionally you don't have to worry about being removed from the station due to programming changes.

Ultimately a podcast should be thought of as an extension of yourself. A podcast is a platform to share your ideas with people in a very personal way. Very much the way people use their blog to convey their thoughts on.

The more open you are and the more fun you have on your show the better the show will be. If you fake it the audience will hear it in your voice and will begin to tune you out.

Bottom line podcasting is your entrance into being a talk show host and entering into show business without breaking the bank (well you can, so be careful). Compared to Radio, podcasting is the least expensive method of breaking into the world of Media and in most cases there are no contracts to sign.

Comparing Podcasting to Broadcasting

The major thing that sets Podcasting apart from its Broadcasting cousin is the breath and width of programming choices. What podcasting is to radio is what Cable TV is to Free TV. Let me explain.

Free TV is very narrow in its scope ABC, NBC, CBS, FOX, PBS and WB along with all the second tier stations. These stations offer 24/7 programming so this means 6 to 16 local free channels worth of programming verses 200 cable channels worth of programming.

You'll note the big three rarely venture far from each other in the types of programming they offer. The reason is simple, these are premium channels that cater to the largest TV watching demographic and they can't afford to steer too far off the beaten track of what has always worked.

On the flip side a cable show is lucky to get a few million viewers whereas a CBS program will garner 5 times that amount of viewers. Think Dancing with the Stars. This is a premium show you won't find this type of show on a cable network as producers just can't afford to create it and air it as they won't get the eyeballs they need to make this type of show work.

Cable/Dish each offer a couple hundred channels or more to choose from and have much less money to throw around as the Big 5. So much of their programming is low cost creations. Note, this is changing with specific channels. These cable channels also run a ton of re-runs verses first airing low re-runs as the big 3.

The big 5 networks/channels have to cater to everyone's interests throughout the day whereas their cable channel counterparts can focus on one idea and make it their niche as in the DIY station which offers 24 hour programming around the subject of Do It Yourself/Home Improvement. These stations may get a few million watchers per day but since they are focused on DIY they can sell ad time to all the DIY type of companies: paint, tools, gardening supplies etc. The cost to network is small since many of the shows are created outside of the network and the only cost to network is air time and internal overhead. The show creators often work deals with sponsors to underwrite their shows which offset their production costs and provide them with a paycheck.

Now let's look at Radio broadcasting. In a major market such as Seattle you have 40 or more stations to choose from between FM and AM. Within these stations you find there is a very narrow type of programming: Sports, Political Talk, Religious programing, Music, NPR. The only time programming changes is on the weekend where the stations sell air time to non traditional programming.

The down side of Broadcasting is the move to remove local hosts and replace them with national hosts. In order to keep costs down, many stations (often owned by very large media companies) offer syndicated programs (much like their TV station counterparts) which costs them very little to nothing. The stations sell local advertising spots around these shows in conjunction with the national network ads. Compare that to paying for actual hosts that cost these station money. In order to make money these stations work hard to stay on top of the ratings by continually tweaking their programing to stay current and keep as many ears stuck to their station as possible. The station programmer will play it safe and keep playing the top 40 or top 100 Hits because it has always worked. The end result is lots of bland programing.

Podcasting, like Cable, can offer thousands of types of shows to choose from compared to a few dozen on your local stations. This allows iTunes to offer national syndicated shows right next to a show about motorcycling or travel. The cost to you is very small and there is very little cost to iTunes as they run ads around your show.

This means two things:

1. You are free to do whatever type of show you want.
2. You will be competing against hundreds if not thousands of shows for ear space and that's a very hard place to start out at.

The good news is you are free to explore your space and do a better job of offering content than what your competitor is offering. And the cost to create a Podcast is far lower than renting air time on your local radio station.

3

Lessons from the World of Broadcasting

You may ask yourself, why do I need to know anything about the world of broadcasting? Well I believe in order to better understand the world of podcasting you should have a rudimentary understanding of what proceeded podcasting. The reason is simple, the more you know about what has worked in the world of broadcasting the better equipped you will be to leverage your podcast platform. The more you know what goes into creating a successful broadcast the more you will know about what goes into creating a successful podcast.

When you think about it, the only thing that has changed is the way you are getting your show in front of listeners. One uses airwaves the other uses the World Wide Web.

Structurally speaking there is no difference in formats as you will soon see. So why not avail yourself to 100 years of broadcasting?

One more thing, getting your show placed onto the airwaves is still a big deal and after reading this book you may wish to take your podcast and get it aired on your local radio station.

In the world of media TV is the biggest with the most eyeballs per any media outlet, Radio is second when you consider a well know syndicated show aired on 200 or more station gets several million daily listeners. That's why sponsors are willing to pay money to have their products sold over these shows whereas they may not be so open to a podcast with several thousand listeners.

The history of Radio Broadcasting dates back to mid to the late 1800's, with the launch of the first commercial radio station in the United States by the name of KDKA.

KDKA received the first license to broadcast live in 1920. By 1922 there were 28 stations broadcasting live in America, two years later by 1924 there were 1,400 stations broadcasting live. Today there are over 10,000 stations. As you can see the rise of radio was swift and it took America and the rest of the world by storm.

Most people outside the media world have no idea how radio works or for that matter how people get to be on the air with their show. I think it might do well for us to step back from podcasting for a moment and learn what takes place in the world of broadcasting so you can apply it to producing a Podcast.

The Five Radio Platforms

In Radio Land there are currently four platforms of radio being made available to the masses:

1. Terrestrial Radio

This Radio platform is the oldest of the four platforms. It dates back to the late 1800's but came to life in 1920. Two classifications under the Terrestrial platform are FM and AM stations. Each of these entities is located in a building which houses a radio transmitter that broadcasts their content via a tall tower also housed on their property or somewhere else usually on a tall hill.

These types of stations must own a license which is tied to a specific bandwidth which they can broadcast their content over. This bandwidth is sent out through the airwaves and received by your radio receiver. The radio receiver receives the stations transmission on a specific bandwidth (channel) which is the bandwidth the station has been allowed to broadcast over. Hence 100.3 signifies the FM bandwidth the station has been allowed to transmit their content across. This bandwidth is attached to a license the station leases from the Federal Communications Commission.

Terrestrial stations have a lot of overhead attached to them: equipment, staff, licensing fees paid to BMI/SESAC to name a few. Terrestrial stations are owned by two types of corporate entities:

1. For profit known as Commercial Radio
2. Non-profit known as Public Radio.

2. Satellite Radio also known as Digital Audio Radio Service (DARS)

DARS was established by the FCC in 1992 by establishing certain segments of radio frequency for satellite broadcast on radio.

An auction was subsequently held and two companies were awarded the license to use these frequencies. American Mobile Radio (later to become XM Radio) paid $93 million for their license, and CD Radio (later to become Sirius Satellite Radio) paid $89 million. These licenses are for 8 years. It is estimated that the entire cost of launching a satellite service is around $1.5 billion.

In the spring of 2001, XM Radio successfully launched its two broadcast satellites: "Rock" and "Roll". In September 2001, XM began the first US digital satellite radio service in two markets: Dallas/Ft.Worth and San Diego. Two months later, XM Radio was launched nationwide.

As of today XM and Sirius are one company listed as SiriusXM which boasts 30 million subscribers and 130 plus channels worth of commercial free content. Netflix copied this model and applied it to offering commercial free Video content on a subscriber based model.

SiriusXM has a lot of overhead including operating very expensive satellites which orbit the globe beaming down the content to satellite equipped radios. They also pay a yearly licensing fee to use a portion of the Radio waves owned by the FCC.

3. Cable Radio

Cable Radio is a concept similar to that of cable TV, bringing radio signals into homes via coaxial cable. It is carried through cable companies who bring Video Content into your home via coaxial cable. Cable Radio Network is the leader in this category who operates 7 channels dedicated to talk radio content. This entity also owns a license to operate these 7 channels.

4. Digital Radio

Digital Radio is the newest platform. These stations are 100% online and typically are streaming (broadcasting) their content 24/7. Online networks that stream their content through the World Wide Web can also be heard on portable devices via applications that interface with your mobile devices. ITunes and Stitcher are two platforms digital stations can be heard over.

5. Short Wave Radio

This type of radio station transmits its content using short wave signals. Short Wave Radio is associated with HAM radio operators and CB'S used in Trucks and law enforcement etc. This type of radio station is not used as a commercial outlet here in the states. It is used in foreign counties especially by pirate stations broadcasting their content into closed countries where radio is owned and operated by the Government such North Korea.

The Two Types of Programming

1. Network Programming

Networks create and air 24/7 "Radio Shows" that are picked up and aired by affiliate stations. These affiliate stations also place their own station produced programs around the national content being aired on their station. You see the exact same thing going on with TV stations. Next time you watch TV notice which of your local stations carry NBC, CBS, ABC and Fox programing and you will see which TV stations are affiliate stations.

2. Independent Programming

These shows or features are developed by the station itself or by an independent entity that in most cases purchases air time from these independent stations to air their shows. Infomercials are done this way as are local religious or pet care shows both of which buy air time on independent stations.

The Two Types of Station Ownerships

1. Privately Owned

These stations are owned by a for profit corporation. The owners may be a single operator or a mega media company who owns several stations. These stations can feature network fed content or independent station created content or a mix of both. They generate revenues through advertising, air rental or both.

2. Publicly Owned

These stations are owned by a not for profit corporation. These stations usually run a mixture of NPR National Public Radio Network content along with station created content by host and guest hosts. In some cases no NPR content is aired just localized content. They generate their income through donations by listeners and corporate donors (who can run short ads or have their name mentioned).

These brick and mortar stations have to pay a yearly licensing fee to FCC in addition to all the costs involved in owning and operating a facility including staff, equipment, tower, transmitter and paid station workers and radio personalities.

Station Clock

All stations run off a clock which is made up of a 60 minute radio clock. Each hour is typically broken into 11 segments. Each segment contains one of the following:

- Show Content (music, talk, event)
- Commercials/Public Service Announcements/Featurettes
- Station Identity
- Traffic
- Weather
- News
- Self-Promotion
- Emergency Announcement

All stations use a clock no matter what type, FM, AM, Cable, Digital, Satellite, public private. All networks run off these clocks. As a matter of fact once a station becomes an affiliate of a network they will design their clock around that of the network so as to make sure to have open time for themselves and the network where they can run local news, ads and content.

Types of Shows

In the world of radio there are three ways to get your show on the radio. They are as follows.

1. Pay to Play

Pay to play means you rent air time from station or network to air your show. Just because someone is on the radio does not mean they get paid directly for being aired. Many times shows pay the station or the Network for the privilege of having their show aired.

All infomercials fall into this category as do religious programming and most weekend programming as well as special interest shows. Keep in mind when you rent air time you may be able to own the entire 55 minutes or 44 minutes depending on station or network. The on air time which consists of 44 minutes is yours to do as you wish. All News Stations give you even less time per hour! But they also offer some of the highest ratings as people tune these type of stations in to hear the latest traffic conditions.

2. Barter

These shows don't have to pay the network or the station for their air time, but they don't own any of the non-show portions of the hour either, it is owned by network or station who sells ad space around the content delivered to them by the programmer. In these cases, the show is offered to stations and if they think it is good enough to draw an audience they will pick it up and air it.

Many shows you hear on your local radio station, as in major personalities, fall into the Barter category. Rush Limbaugh is a barter show who gets paid by the Radio Network he works for. The network makes money by generating revenue through national sponsors who underwrite the show. His network works to place his show on as many affiliate stations as possible. The more stations he is aired on the more money the network (syndicator) can charge their sponsors.

The local affiliates stations like this type of show because they don't have to pay a local personality, they garner a large audience base and they can sell ad space around the show to local advertisers who wish to reach Rush fans.

3. Paid

These personalities actually get paid by the hour to work for the station or network. All Music DJ's, local talk show hosts and News personalities get paid by the hour. In most of these cases, these on air personalities are given a contract of a 1 to 3 year period of time. This way if the host or hosts don't get the ratings the station wants, they can let them go at the end of the contract.

As I said earlier many stations are owned by huge corps that only care about making money where independent stations are often owned and operated by true enthusiasts who operate at a near loss in order to stay in the game. Major corps don't care about the content being aired on their stations as long as the station is generating a profit. Thus, when you see major layoffs at a local TV or radio station, it's often because the parent company who owns the local station wants to reduce the highest paid personalities and replace them with lower paid personalities.

The point is this, in traditional radio either you pay to be aired or you're lucky to get aired for free or even luckier and get paid directly by the station or network. You are always left to the whims of the station owner or radio network. One day you are on top the next day the format is changed and you're out of a job.

The beauty of podcasting is you don't have to be a pawn in a larger game of chess being played by corporate heads. You are in total control of what you do and how much money you can make or not make. You are free to leverage your show as you see fit. For a small price you can air your show.

Expenses range from your web hosting fee to possible service fees related to being able to Podcast. Equipment to build a studio will be the biggest investment. But, these costs are far lower than renting air time on a station or network. Keep in mind being on radio does have its benefits.

Now that we have looked at the various radio structures and the ways people get paid or not paid let's turn our attention to the various types of formats commonly aired on radio which can be applied to podcasting.

Categories of Programing

Service

Service is a new description used by the radio industry which describes shows that offer a service to the listener verses pure entertainment or news. Most of these shows have products and services they promote through their show. In many cases these shows Pay to Play but not all do. The following are the top three in the Service category: Dave Ramsey, Clark Howard and Kim

Kamando each of these shows are aired on hundreds of station across the US.

Political/Conservative Talk

These shows are just that. These shows are host driven talk shows typically focusing on what is happening within the Social-political landscape. They do play-by-play commentary of local, regional, national and international government and society. The top three voices in the conservative talk arena are Rush Limbaugh, Sean Hannity and Michael Medved. All of them are heard on hundreds of stations across the US and are paid by the Syndication Company they work for.

Business

Networks such as Bloomberg Radio Network are dedicated to business and financial advice. Many of the shows on this network are Service Shows paid to air their content.

Sports

Sports Networks such as ESPN or FOX are 100% dedicated to covering sports. There are dozens of nationally syndicated sports talk hosts and thousands of local sports talk hosts heard on network affiliate stations and independent stations across the United States. Sports programming is very popular among men. In the greater Seattle Market there are 6 or more stations covering sports. This doesn't even include local and national sporting events broadcast on non-sports related stations.

Shock Jock

There are hundreds of shock jocks on the airwaves one of the first in this genera is Howard Stern, king of smut talk radio. Stern makes millions promoting the porn industry and various celebrities yet his popularity has allowed him to garner a spot on Americas Got Talent! Only in Hollywood would this ever happen. None the less he is the true pioneer of the Shock Jock Genre and as such maintains his position as king of smut right up there with Heffner and Flynt.

Self Help
This type of show focuses on helping people with their physical and emotional needs. Dr Laura, New Life Live and Focus on the Family are three of the biggies heard daily on hundreds of stations.

Christian
This type of show focuses on helping people with their spiritual health and living out their Christian faith. Insights for Family Living, Family Life Today and Key Life are three major players in the Christian Broadcasting world. Each of these shows is aired on hundreds of stations around the world often paying for the air time they're heard on. They raise money through donations.

Catholic
The Catholic Church has its own version of NPR/affiliate stations that carry 24/7 programing from a Catholic point of view. Supported by the church and donors.

Progressive Talk
This type of programming consists of New Age teaching/Healing Arts to left leaning/progressive talk shows.

Music
This type of programming consists of music only. Programming ranges from Jazz to Country and all points in between. Some of these stations are manned by live DJ's, while others are 100% automated such as Jack FM.

News
This is type of programming consists of news all day long interspersed with Weather and traffic reports and brief special interest features. There are even all traffic stations.

Public Radio/NPR

This is a governmental owned network which airs its content on affiliate stations (publically owned). NPR programming is created through their headquarters and is also provided by independent producers. Show producers fortunate enough (Garrison Keillor) to get their show aired on NPR have it made, because NPR programming has the widest reach of all programing in America reaching many hundreds of affiliate stations and millions of Americans and Canadians alike.

Special Interest

This type of programming can be anything from fishing, motorcycling, auto racing or shooting guns. These shows typically fall into the pay to play category even if they are not selling anything.

Infomercial

This type of program is designed to sell products and services by the hosts. This ranges from supplements to Mortgages and Investing and all points in between. Nearly every commercial AM station in America opens up their weekend programming to Infomercials.

The Power of Infomercials

Because these shows have to purchase air time from a station or network they typically are free to say and do whatever they wish related to selling you on their products. The job of the host(s) is to sell you their service or product. It's an hour of telling you why their products will solve all your problems.

These types of shows are money in the pocket for station owners and less risky then trying to find paying sponsors to underwrite a Barter Program. It's good for the station owner and show owner who both end up with money in their pocket.

Please note many of the hosts of these types of shows don't like to be called infomercials and have coined a new term called Service Radio Shows. This is a trend within the world of marketing. Rather than state the obvious they change it sound more sophisticated. The following is an example: Used cars are now referred to as previously owned cars.

The point is Service Shows (infomercials) have been popular for a long time and aren't going away anytime soon. This format may lend itself well for what you wish to accomplish. If you offer information listeners can apply to their life you will become a trusted "expert" in their eyes.

As an expert you will be building trust and people who trust you will also trust you enough to purchase your products.

With this in mind, let's take a look at some of the longest running most successful shows in the traditional radio sector. Keep in mind these are pioneers who are at the top of their game. Chances are good they have their category locked up at least on the stations that carry them which is still very small compared to the overall stations available in the US.

The Kings and Queen of Infomercials the Best in Service Radio

Dave Ramsey

Dave Ramsey is king of the Service Radio Sector. His specialty is money management for dummies. Dave began his career renting airtime on a local station where he used the platform to sell people on using his money management services. He has grown his show from a local show to a nationwide phenomenon.

Dave basically stole, or as he likes to say adopted, the Larry Burkett Mantel (The real pioneer in money management radio) and then injected his own sense of humor and sensibilities into it. Where as Larry operated a non profit "ministry" Dave's company even though broadcast over hundreds of Christian stations, is a 100% for profit corporation.

Dave understands his core audience as Middle American Christians who need help understanding how to get out of debt and live on a budget. His focus has always had a strong underlying Christian emphasis without being overly preachy.

Dave has built up an empire based on his teachings and products which consisting of: books, courses, seminars and other fee based products. He also writes a syndicated column published in various Christian and general audience newspapers and publications. He has appeared on the cover of Success Magazine and other financial magazines. He also makes appearances on various TV and Radio shows.

Dave is by far the king of Infomercials and the wealthiest, as well. He has a huge number of people working for him. He has figured out how to profit from radio and podcasting.

Dave has a team of paid sales people who contact companies who operate where his show is being aired and creates affiliate sponsorship programs with them. They actually end up paying for his air time as Dave buys his air time on most stations he is aired on. In return Dave let's these companies advertise on his show (during local breaks). Dave will promote these services with in show shout outs.

Dave's reputation sells products because people trust him and will purchase from anyone attached to him even if those companies are more expensive than their competitors! Celebrity pays big dividends especially when you know how to harness your services and products and package them into bite sized products people can't get enough of.

I won't even get into the details of how he has harnessed thousands of volunteers who promote his courses in their local churches (which attendees must pay for).

Dave is a true pioneer of building a hard core non-paid tribe of volunteers who proactively promote his products while Dave whistles Dixie, all the way to the bank!

Clark Howard

Clark is nationally syndicated show who offers consumer related help to callers to his show. Unlike Dave, Howard doesn't have a legion of followers who promote his products and services. He offers much of his help for nothing. He does have a paid staff that goes to bat for you. Clark has been fortunate to make a living at what he loves doing for over 20 years. We even called and used his teams help with a consumer related issue and they helped us at no charge.

Kim Kamando

Kim is the Tech Goddess of the airwaves who helps millions of listeners with their technology problems each and every weekend. She makes money off her website services and products along with the money she earns from her affiliate partnerships and advertisers of the companies she promotes on her show such as Carbonite and Go Daddy. She even started her own self syndication company which has done well for her to place her onto the airwaves in many markets around the United States.

These three epitomize the power of the Service Sector. Each one is at the top of their sector. I would highly recommend you looking them up and listening to how they do their shows, viewing their websites and checking out how they do what they do as you can learn a lot by doing so.

Keep in mind each have employees who work for them, something many of you won't have in place when you first begin to podcast. Who knows, maybe one of these these days you will!

There are dozens if not hundreds of regional and national shows who follow what these giants are doing and they too are making a living at selling their products and services through their show.

The 7 Ingredients to Creating a Top Performing Service Show

1) Host interacts with listeners through a live call in format
2) Host has the ability to create trust within their audience

3) Host offers information people need and want
4) Host has distinct personality, they don't copy someone else
5) Host understands their audience and caters to them
6) Host is an expert in their specific field
7) In most cases hosts are first in category or did a better job beating out their competitor to become first (there is always opportunity for new talent since not any one host is on more than a fraction of all radio stations that dot the US.

You may not be the first in your category but that shouldn't stop you from working at being number one in your niche category. If you're willing to learn and emulate what these giants have done you'll be able to build a media platform that is a powerful way to promote yourself. It will also provide you with the opportunity to leverage your podcast into the broadcast arena should you wish to. Above all, your show can be considered an integral component of your marketing strategy.

If you emulate what works for these Top Guns and don't go too far astray you won't go wrong. Listen to these shows and learn from how they do it and follow there examples. But please be your self.

Pay to Play

Have you ever wondered why there are so many weekend shows trying to sell you something? The answer is they pay the station or network to air their show. Here's how they do it.

1. They purchase unsold air time at a very low cost. These marketers seek out low rate air time from stations within a given market demographic. Rather than pay top dollar they find out remnant time and air their show at these times.
2. They purchase large enough blocks of air time so they get a discounted price from station or network.

3. They purchase air time over several stations. Most radio stations in any given local area are owned by the same company, so they can give breaks to advertisers and producers who wish to purchase air time across all their platforms at a discounted price.
4. THEY KNOW WHO THERE PERFECT CUSTOMER IS so they air their show on stations with high percentages of people who fit their perfect demographic.
5. Split sales with station. Sometimes a company will pitch a station on letting them have a specific amount of air time at no charge in return for a percentage of sales they make from the their show. These marketers understand the value of a customer and have no problem giving away the initial sale price. These marketers know a high percentage of these buyers will be repeat customers and that's where they will make their money from.

Lastly, if these business entities fail to hit their sales goals, they yank the show ASAP and move onto another station until they find their perfect audience who buys their products. So when you hear a long running infomercial on your favorite station, understand they are getting lots of sales. Why reinvent the wheel as long as it works don't stop doing what you are doing.

Mind you, the podcast world is a bit different but you can still build a following and test your message over a period of time using various offers designed to get people to sign up for your email form.

4

Podcast vs Broadcast
Comparing Podcasting to Traditional Broadcasting

I don't have to tell you that as a podcaster you will be swimming in an ocean full of other casters. Just as in the broadcasting world where there are an estimated 10,000 plus radio stations across the United States. On the web there are just as many podcasters as there are hosts of radio shows. The bad news is you will be vying for the ears of an audience who is already consuming their favorite shows. The question for you is, how will they find you?

The difference between podcasting and broadcasting is your audience is no longer limited to a local station that reaches a specific region instead it's as broad and wide as the entire globe! The following is list of positives and negatives to both platforms.

The Strength of Local Radio

- Built in station audience
- Localized targeted audience
- Ability to funnel people to localized seminars
- Ability to offer localized services
- You get Arbitron ratings (which go a long way to move your show up the rungs of regular radio and to bring on sponsors)

- Ability to build credibility in your region which open doors to various local entities
- Ability to create Home Town Hero status
- Ability to bring in local sponsors
- Ability to bring on local guests
- Ability to partner with local talent
- Ability to partner with local businesses
- Ability to partner with key people within your community
- Who wish to leverage your show to reach their customers
- Ability to spread the cost to these localized partners

The Weakness of Local Radio

- The high cost to rent air time
- Low Arbitron ratings (because your show is aired on a low rated station)
- Localized audience
- Possible contracts
- Must show up in a studio or send in production to station every week
- Limited time (Some stations rent 22 min per 60 min period)

The Power of Podcasting

- Low cost of entry,
- Ability to reach a world wide audience
- Ability to reach a localized audience
- Ability to share your show through all the online portals
- Ability to syndicate show on numerous podcast portals
- Ability to link show to guest websites
- Ability to link show to Affiliate partners
- Ability to grow your audience at your own pace
- Portability

- On demand (this means people can listen to the show when they want to, not on a scheduled basis)

The Drawbacks of Podcasting

- Traditional media users aren't as familiar with podcasting
- Legitimacy factor. Podcasting doesn't have the status, traditional radio does
- No built in audience you get with a radio station
- Limited reach both local and national
- Responsible for your own production duties verses a station who handles it for you. If you hire a producer they can handle the production process for you
- You will need a website to promote your show unlike radio station who may offer you space on their page
- Cost of webmaster to create website or podcast portal
- Studio and equipment costs
- Steep learning curve to using recording software as compared to walking into a professional studio
- Poor sound quality (lack of knowledge leads podcasters to create sub standard sounding shows)
- Lack of guidance and direction can lead to burn out
- Inability to take live calls from audience (yes there are ways to do this but they cost money)
- No set schedule verses radio which has a set schedule and forces people to tune you in or miss the show

5

Podcast Programming
Podcast Channel Categories

When you go to create a membership in iTunes, Podomatic or Blog talk Radio you will be asked what major category and then sub category you will want to be listed under. The following is a list of categories/subcategories found on Podomatic.

Arts
Design, Fashion, Beauty, Food, Literature, Performance Arts, Spoken Word, Visual Arts

Business
Business News, Careers, Investment, Management/Marketing, Shopping

Comedy

Education
Education Technology, Higher Ed, K-12, Language, Training

Games/Hobbies
Automotive, Aviation, Hobbies, Other Games, Video Games

Government/Orgs
Local, National, Non-Profit, Regional

Health
All Health, Fitness, Diet, Self-Help, Sexuality

Kids/Family

Music
Alt, Blues, Country, Easy Listening, Electronic, Folk, Freedom, Hip-Hop/Rap, Inspirational, Jazz, Latin, Rock

News/Politics
Conservative, Liberal

Religion/Spirituality
Buddhism, Christianity, Hinduism, ISLAM, Judaism, Other, Spirituality

Science/Medical
Medicine, Natural Sciences, Social Sciences

Society/Culture
Gay/Lesbian, History, Personal Journal, Philosophy, Places/Travel

Sports/Recreation
Armature, College/School, Outdoor, Professional

TV/Film

Technology
Gadgets, IT News, Pod casting, Software Technology

As you can see, there are numerous categories and subcategories so you will have to decide which one will serve you in reaching the type of audience you want to reach. For example you may not be an auto show but it is the closest thing to Motorcycling you can find under the general category of games and hobbies. This will most likely be the category and sub category you choose.

As I've said before, unlike radio, podcasting offers better narrow casting so you can reach the audience most interested in your particular content.

Let's say you create a weekly show about gardening this means you will place your show under the broad category of Games/Hobbies and the Subcategory of Other. Under this category/subcategory you may be competing against 20 other gardening shows. You might think this is bad but it's not.

Think about the DIY TV Network which provides 24/7 programming around Do It Yourself subjects such as fixing up an old house or gardening. The cool thing is the people who tune in these shows are hungry for more shows about the same subject. This means they are likely to check out your show also featured under this category.

Competition isn't bad, it's actually good because the more shows about a specific topic the bigger draw it is to listeners. So find a category and run with it and know that people who listen to similar shows like yours will check your show out as well. If they like it they will add it to their play list.

One last point, you can always experiment as I did, to find out which category helps you grow faster.

Program Formats

Under show categories you have various formats to choose from. Formats are not to be confused with types of programming. These formats fall into one of the following:

Live Format

Live means just that, you have a designated time you are on each week or each day. Even if you don't have a studio to let people call you, you can leverage twitter or live chat technology so people can interact with you and your guests while you're on air.

Prerecorded Format

This type of show is recorded on one date and aired on another date. The majority of NPR falls into this type of show. The majority of TV falls into this category with the exception of Sports, News and the occasional special.

Guest Driven Format

These types of shows are focused on interviewing guests. Think Book Talk or Authors Corner or Charlie Rose as in TV. Without a guest the host would have very little to bring to the table.

Host Driven Format

These types of shows revolve around the singular host and will only occasionally bring on a guest or allow for caller interaction. Rush Limbaugh is a perfect example. Rush rarely, if ever, brings on a guest and is very limited in call in's by listeners. Yet he holds court for 3 hours a day 5 days a week and is still one of the top shows in broadcasting. Rush is the master of Talk Radio and it reflected in his paycheck!

Caller Driven Format

These types of shows thrive on caller interaction with the host or hosts. It's all about getting people calling into the show and sharing their opinions with hosts. You never know where these types of shows will go which makes them attractive to an audience.

Mix Format

Most talk shows fall into this category. These shows are live and allow for Call Ins. They bring on guests and some even bring in their producer or news people to join them during portions of the show.

Determining the Length for Your Show

There are no hard and fast rules in the world of podcasting when it comes to the length of your finished podcast. This is evidenced by the various lengths of podcasts being produced today. On the other hand, there are hard and fast rules in the broadcast world.

In my opinion, it's better to error on the side of tradition than to reinvent the wheel. Therefore, I prefer to produce shows that align with the traditional radio broadcast format listed below.

- .90 second block of time
- 5 minute block of time
- 15 minute block of time
- 30 minute block of time
- 60 minute block of time
- 2 hour block of time
- 3 hour block of time

If you stay within these formats you won't go wrong. By keeping your show to the same length found on traditional radio it lets people relate to your show better as they are already accustomed to Radio Shows. It will automatically help you sound more professional.

When you watch TV or listen to the radio, you notice they do their programming in 30 minute increments. The Hog Radio Show which I produce is 55:50 minutes because it's designed to air on an online radio station. I have built in breaks for Ads and the remaining time is owned by station.

A Lesson from the Retail World

It used to be if someone opened up a store on a street they would get only so much traffic. What retailers soon discovered was the more stores built next to each other the greater amount of traffic generated. Why you might ask? Because the person shopping for shoes may not come back until they needed a new pair of shoes. On the other hand, if the shoe store is next to the grocery store the people who came to buy groceries would be more likely to pop into the shoe store as they were already in town. That's how the shopping district was born. You see this reflected in countries around the world, including shopping malls.

Today malls are still major destination zones for shoppers. But they have some competition in the form of large stand alone retailers the likes of Wall Mart or Fred Meyer. But even these "All in one" style stores have taken a page our of the Mall marketing manual and have begun selling parking lot space to other non competing business as a way to draw more people to their stores.

Today it's common practice to build strip malls surrounding big box retail stores. Malls have even begun incorporated this into their development plans through the process of retrofitting their current building with additional outside mini marketplaces located at various entrances to the Mall.

Apply this thinking to the podcast world and use the iTunes/Podomatic category choices to your benefit, to get your show in front of people who listen to similar shows that fall into the same category. If it works for retailers, it will work for you. It's a simple, yet powerful way to get your show in front of the people most interested in your topic. It's called synergy.

Synergy means the sum is greater than the parts. Use it to your benefit.

One more thing you can do, and that's to create alliances with other podcasters and be guests on each others shows for the purposes of cross promoting each other. This is what malls do.

A mall houses a bunch of shops and makes it easy for each shop to be in one place and thus when a customer comes in to shop at one store they have to pass by all the other shops. When one store has a promotion all the stores benefit.

Many malls do collective events designed to bring people into the mall such as special Holiday events. Radio stations do the same thing. These entities will hold an event where all the hosts come together. These events provide a forum where each national and local host can pitch their books and greet their fans.

Putting on an event costs money so they usually charge a small fee to cover expenses for renting the auditorium.

The point of me sharing this information is to show you the power of collaboration that can take place between a group hosts should you decided to partner up for an in person or online event.

Without Watson There Would be No Holms, The power of Two

Do you have someone you can partner with to co-host your show? Having a co-host often makes for a more entertaining show (in most cases). Having a partner spreads the responsibility between two or more persons. By having a co-host you always work off each other's energy which helps to keep the show flowing and less apt to drag along.

A co-host can also play the part of the listener by prodding the host with questions. This is very important for an infomercial type show, where you are selling something.

Chances are good, you probably know someone who would love to sit in with you, either in person or over an internet phone line such as Skype. Special Note: Skype charges for the use of their service.

In the world of entertainment there are a lot of famous pairs who play off each other. Sherlock had his trusty side kick Dr Watson who faithfully recorded all the cases. If he didn't we would never know about Sherlock's famous crimes. You have Laurel and Hardy, Bing Crosby and Bob Hope, Jerry Lewis and Dean Martin. Bat Man and Robin and for TV shows you have Starsky and Hutch, Hunter and McCall, Simon and Simon, all the way back to the Lone Ranger and Tonto.

These partnerships were the mainstay of television for decades before the team approach was adopted which is found in many of today's cop shows. There are numerous morning and afternoon radio show host teams.

Some shows have gone with a team approach as have many TV shows but the duo is still a very powerful formula for a popular show format. The old saying "two is company" is a powerful combination in the world of entertainment.

The reason is pretty simple: There is power in numbers; there are more chances for personalities to play off each other. The Hog Radio Show has always been based on Walt and Steve. We are the show plus the personalities we interview. We have also incorporated a third person from time to time who comes in and joins us at the studio table, making it a threesome. Typically the third person does less talking but when they do it's always gold because they add a third dimension we wouldn't have otherwise.

In the Infomercial category one personality plays the part of the novice or student who sets up the questions for the teacher or expert (that's you). The other personality is the salesperson or expert who answers all the questions and pitches the product. By using this format the student personality pulls out of you things you may not think about on your own. They can also be the guide making sure you stay on topic and don't stray too far down the rabbit hole.

Note: often interview/infomercial style podcasts are preplanned with pre-made questions. This lets the host (salesperson/expert) field the questions in such a way that they want. Which leads us right into the following format and that's the question and answer format.

Question and Answer Format

Infomercials are king of the question and answer formatted shows which have sold billions in products and services. Keep in mind, these question and answer infomercial shows are completely scripted and recorded well ahead of the actual air date. These shows design their intro, body and ending to lead you through the sales funnel and out the other side where they hope you will do one of the following things:

- Stay put and begin listening to the show (get hooked)
- Come back to listen next day or next week
- Call their toll free number to get more info
- Sign up for upcoming seminar
- Purchase products
- Visit their website to get more information, sign up for their free: Seminar, Sample, Special Report
- Call in and ask the Expert questions regarding the information they are talking about. (If it is a live show).
- Cause you to change the station (This is good, because they have already pre-screened you as not worth going after).

The coolest thing about an infomercial is it is designed to thin out the herd ahead of time. It's designed to reach only the people who qualify for said services. Yes, I said qualify because in the world of sales if you don't prequalify people, you will waste time and money chasing people who see no need for your services. Infomercials are powerful platforms to prequalify and then push those who do qualify into your sales funnel.

Best way to understand this format is to listen to the weekend shows on your AM dial to see what I am talking about. You might consider recording a handful of them so can duplicate their process. These shows are aired all over America so you should have no problem finding and listening to them.

All infomercials use a track-able toll free number or landing page. This way they can track each stations response rate. If after a month lets say of being on a specific station they don't get the results they want they will yank the show and move it to a another station.

Infomercials are excellent lead generation tools in your marketing arsenal. A well designed show of this type builds trust by building familiarity and offering useful information. These shows give these hosts (Marketers) a 44 minute platform to educate listeners on all the reasons they are the better choice over their competitors.

WARNING, Don't Use Copyrighted Music in Your Podcasts

In the world of online stealing, where almost everyone listens and downloads music they didn't pay for, you might assume its okay to use someone's music in your podcast without getting their permission. You would be assuming the wrong thing. The following is a list of facts you need to know about using music in your podcast:

- You can be sued for the use of copyrighted music.
- You cannot use any part of copyrighted music, not even for a short bumper, without permission from the creator or owner of the material.
- Radio Stations pay a blanket royalty fee for the use of any music they use to the collectors of royalty fees namely BMI and ASCAP.

The good news for you is there is a way around this problem. The following is a list of ways to use music and avoid being sued:

- Purchase Royalty Free Music from an online provider.
- Find Independent Artists who wants their music heard and work a deal with them. I suggest you create a form they sign which waives their rights to any compensation and gives you permission to play their music without recourse.
- Create your own music.

Full disclosure I use music given to me by independent artists so I do not have to pay royalty fees.

Building a Radio Ready Show

For those who have major goals such as getting your show aired on traditional radio stations, you will need to work with a station or network to set up your show according to their radio clock. Radio clocks are different from network to network but most are close enough that a savvy producer can manipulate the show to fit a variety of network/station formats. I go into greater detail on setting up a clock in a later chapter but for now let me show you a couple of examples:

- 30 Minute Radio show or slot means you get 22 to 24 minutes of air time in this half hour of time, the rest belongs to the station. Your time will be broken into segments. These segments will have to be saved as individual MP3 files which you upload to the station portal.
- 60 Minute slot means you get 42 minutes of air time. Again you will need to break your show into several segments which will be uploaded to station.

If you don't believe me, just watch an hour long show shown on Netflix. What you'll notice is that a 60 minute show you typically watch on Network TV turns out to be 42 to 44 minutes run time. Radio is exactly the same.

For my online radio station I send them an MP3 File which is 55 minutes in length. When our show was being aired on a brand new radio network (that unfortunately for everyone went under) I would send them four individual MP3 Files each representing a segment of the hour.

The point is this, when you go to work with a station or network you will need to follow their clock otherwise your show won't be aired.

I understand the radio world and should you wish to you're your show aired on the radio, I can help you.

Adding Commercial Breaks

If you plan to do radio you will need to create Ad breaks as part of your show. If you don't plan to be on the radio, it's still a good idea to add commercial breaks to your show for future sponsors you might bring on. This means more work up front but if you set up a template in your audio software you can build these breaks into the show which remain there week in and week out.

You may think people don't want breaks but in reality breaks can be helpful. The mind of the listener often needs times to dissect what is being said and a break gives the brain a chance to do this.

Breaks build anticipation for the next segment to be aired – just like TV shows. Yes, I agree there are too many commercials but someone has to pay for the programming and it might as well be the advertisers on your show.

What do you use to fill in the additional unsold ad space? Your own self promotions such as "Hey this is Big John and I want to invite you to sign up for our free monthly newsletter"… or you can run Public Service Announcements (PSA). PSA's as they're called can be found at the AD Council website.

When I first started in Radio, I didn't have any sponsors so the engineer helped me be teaching me about Public Service Announcements which I've used ever sense to fill unsold ad space.

Rule of Thumb

When determining how long to make your show always keep it shorter. It's far better to leave listeners wanting more than overstaying your time with them. There is little reason you should go over an hour a week per show unless you are being paid to create and air your show. Remember, for every hour on air there are several off air hours writing outlines, contacting guests, recoding the show, editing the show, producing and uploading the show to the various online feeds.

Unlike your paid radio counterparts who have producers, engineers and call screener, you as a podcaster have to do it all on your own. So don't burn yourself out trying to do more than you need to.

6

Personal Development
You Have to Have a Why, Before You Can Fly

In order to create a great podcast you need a game plan. Your game plan spells out what you want to accomplish and how you're going to do it. The following section is designed to help you not only assess the why behind your desire to go into podcasting but to help you get the most out of your Podcast platform..

Many of us go into podcasting because we love radio. We love the medium and the opportunities our show allots us, such as meeting new people through our show. We hope to make money someday but the reality is, most never do. Others use it as an extension of their marketing strategy.

Whatever the reason you go into podcasting keep in mind you will do well if you're honest in all your dealings and deliver more than is expected. You may think podcasting can replace your other forms of advertising if wont. The reality is, it will require a lot from you so keep this in mind as you think through the idea of podcasting.

Podcasting Your Personal Advertising Platform

Advertising is nothing more than letting people know you have a service to offer and why you're different from everyone else who is offering a similar service. Your show can be an important advertising platform. Many types of businesses use the air waves to raise awareness of what they're doing. Mortgage Brokers to Bible Teachers, Doctors to Mechanics leverage the airwaves to promote their businesses.

Your show will most likely be about you and your services. Unlike a 30 second commercial a 30 or 60 minute show gives you a huge amount of time to share yourself with an audience.

Time + sharing = Familiarity. The more time spent with you, the more familiar an audience becomes with you. The more familiar an audiences becomes with you, the greater trust they will have in you.

In the world of selling, trust goes a very long way towards creating ongoing sales. That's what makes podcasting such a powerful medium to "sell yourself" to your potential clients.

In the world of online selling where consumers have been conditioned to search for the cheapest price, a podcast can transform your commodity product, into a must have product.

Podcasts are designed to educate people on the merits of a product or service, something a Google Ad, can't do.

Information packed podcasts are excellent permission marketing platforms. A podcast can transform those very same price shoppers into fans. Why? Because as I explained above, once a person trusts in you, they will be much more likely to buy from you, regardless of price.

The same person, who will spend an hour trying to save a dollar, will gladly spend an hour listening to a podcast about a topic, they're passionate about. This means, rather than putting all your money into Google ads and compete on low pricing you can put your efforts into creating a cool show. The show is where you can sell your products at a much higher price.

People who spend time with you, are more likely to trust you. Let me show you what I am talking about.

Building Trust to Build Bridges

Let's say you own a coaching service that offers services to mid sized companies. You decide to promote yourself by doing a series of Podcasts on how to have confidence in the workplace.

1. You use this platform to build expert position for yourself.
2. You push listeners to your Landing Page, with offers for free reports. This is where you collect their email.
3. You contact a Trade Publication/Magazine that caters to your demographic and invite the editor on to chat about workplace confidence. In return, they agree to promote the interview (podcast) on their website and in their magazine.
4. You offer to write a series of articles for the magazine as long as you can promote your weekly podcast.

Soon your name becomes well known and when a company begins looking for an expert in workplace confidence your name appears. You can do this with similar topics. The point is, your podcast sets you apart and opens doors for further "free" promotion, your non podcasting competitors can't get.

That's the power of podcasting. It lets a no name become somebody. It allows people to share their knowledge at a very low entrance price as compared to renting air time on a radio station or running an ad in a trade publication or major magazine.

Now that we've covered what makes for a great show, let's find out what makes you a great candidate for being a great podcaster. In order to do this, you must discover what makes you, you.

What's your USP?

In the world of advertising and marketing the key to helping an agency sell your product is to understand what makes your product so unique. This is called the Unique Selling Proposition. It may be as simple as highlighting something that is common to all products but has not been mentioned in advertising before. Such phrases as Mountain Fresh Water or Champaign of all Beers are slogans that have sold a lot of beer.

Your USP is what sets you apart from everyone else. To become successful you can't be something someone already is! Instead you must carve out your own niche, your own personality, your own slant, your own brand. Let me give you an example:

Marketing Lesson Form the World of Beer.

Budweiser King of the Beers has been battling it out against Miller the Champaign of Beers. Both these brands have been slugging it out for a very long time.

What sets Bud apart from Miller is the use of rice in its list of ingredients making for a slightly dryer taste compared to Miller who uses more traditional ingredients. None the less both brands were based on traditional German Lager recipes a favorite among German immigrants who came to America during the 1800's. This light liquid gold was the mainstay of nearly every brewer in the United States for close to 100 years excluding prohibition times. The bottom line is there is very little distinction between these brewers.

Bud and Miller became household names by building huge distribution systems and applying the science of mass marketing. Suffice it to say their brew found its way into every market place within the US and beyond.

Up until the early 1980's all beer sold in America and Canada tasted pretty much the same. With only a few import exceptions this Lager Style beer took up nearly all the cooler space at the local grocer. That is, until an upstart by the name of Red Hook Brewery began brewing up their own version of what they thought was a better tasting beer.

After a number of trials and errors the brewers at Red Hook created a brew that started to catch on with the new generation of beer drinkers who had already begun to move away from Folgers Coffee and were demanding Starbucks style coffee. These same consumers were tired of the same old same old and longed for a more robust flavored beer. Hence Red Hook took advantage of this change in taste by younger consumers (Baby Boomers) and quickly moved their products into the marketplace.

Soon everyone is Seattle and the greater Washington State marketplace started to purchase Red Hook beer. They weren't alone as other upstarts began crafting their own version of beer.

In the past, the beer space was devoted to Miller, Budweiser and several other major brands with about 2 feet allotted to maybe a hand full of specialty imports. Today Miller, Bud and other Major Labels have less shelf space and more space has been devoted to craft beers.

How did this happen? Long story short Baby Boomers wanted more choices than their parents, they weren't happy with status quo. Today's baby boomers and their children want even more choices thus as long as there are people who want more choices there will be new beers, hard ciders and various other newly produced hard spirits and wines added to a huge adult beverage market.

Apply this to podcasting. Today's younger tech savvy generation wants variety and they want it when they wish to consume it! Hence the birth of on-demand services which podcasting falls directly in-line with.

People are no longer relegated to what their local AM/FM dial has to offer. Today millions of consumers have turned to the Web and alternative outlets to get their media. They are getting their media via mobile devices, PC's, Radio and other digital platforms. They want programing that speaks to their interests, not that of the networks and station programmers.

As a podcaster, think of yourself as a Craft Brewer – what is going to set you apart from everyone else within your category? Remember beer is beer, it's not wine and it's not milk. The upstart brewers didn't market themselves to wine drinkers nor to milk drinkers but to beer drinkers. They understood the suds business and did all they could to leverage this platform and push their new product into the beer drinking world and build their brands. With this in mind let's find out who you are.

Who Are You?

Who are you? First and foremost a podcast is an Audio Show! Yep, that's who you are. What aren't you? You're not a video show and possibly you're not a live show that allows people to call in or interact with you while you do your podcast. So make sure to stick with what you are. If you want to have a Live Show Feel do your show in such a way it comes across as one.

Understand your medium (that's why I spend so much time on examples of best in class in your medium) so you can maximize it to your benefit. Even if you want to go into video down the road you must see yourself as an audio show. Once you have that understanding you will then have to understand what program category you will be listed under so you can stay within this niche and not stray outside it.

If you're a sports show then become the most unique sports show you can be. If you're a business show then become the most unique business show you can. The following is a list of things to ask yourself and help you craft your USP.

- What makes you unique?
- What sets your show or you apart from all the other people within your category?
- What makes you different?
- What are you selling that is different or can be packaged differently?
- What makes your service different or unique?
- Why should anyone trust you?
- What is it that drives you?

- What unique qualities make your products stand out from all the others in your category?
- What are your passions and do they have anything to do with what you are selling?
- How can you bottle up your enthusiasm and pour it into your podcast?
- Do you wish to sell something or just entertain?
- Is your platform a means to an end or an end to itself?
- What positive things have people said about the way you operate your business?
- What personal attributes have people positively commented on?
- What negative attributes have people said turned them off to you?
- What makes you, you?
- Are you offering the exact same thing as someone else? If so, how can you showcase your different approach or different ingredients or different methods to set yourself apart from other like-minded shows or service providers?

Keep in mind, beer makers, wine makers and whiskey makers all use the same basic ingredients. It's the way they use these ingredients or the way these ingredients are handled that changes the outcome. These slight differences in the production and use of the ingredients, is what sets them apart from their competitors. The same can be said about YOU!

Maybe you want to be a show about a medical practice. If that's the case, what makes your practice different from all the other hundreds of other practices competing for your patient base?

Is it the way you treat your patients? Is it some new ways of doing things that have yet to catch on? There has to be something that sets you apart from the other medical shows.

Look at the shows you like to listen to most on the radio and in the podcast world. Why do you like listening to them? What makes one host different from the others? As you examine the various shows you like the most, make mental note of it, even write it down. Then ask yourself if you can create the very same aura about yourself using your USP.

A great book that may help you figure out how to set yourself and your business apart from the pack is The 22 Immutable Laws of Marketing.

So again let me ask you:
- What is the purpose behind you producing a Podcast?
- Build trust - which you use to get people to buy your services and or products?
- Build an email list – which you use to sell them something?
- Build expert positioning – so you can get booked as a speaker, host, spokesperson or pitch person to sell books and other info materials?
- Build celebrity – which you use to get booked onto TV/Radio Shows which opens more doors for paid hosting positions?
- Change the world one listener at a time?

When you have these questions nailed down you are on the right track to launch a successful show.

7

Setting up your Studio
Congratulations you're a producer now!

Have you heard of the term producer, you probably have but really didn't think about it. For those not familiar with the term producer look at the credits of every TV show and movie and you will see producer listed, possibly a number of them. So what does the producer do? It depends but for the most part the producer is responsible for making everything come together. Picture the producer as a General Contractor who oversees the building of a house He is in charge of hiring sub-contractors and making sure the job is completed on budget and on time.

The producer oversees the creation of a media property. That media property can be in the form of a record, radio show, movie, TV show, audio book, play and yes, a podcast. The producer is responsible for producing the podcast which includes finding talent and staff to promoting the show to pitching the show to media entities whom you may wish to partner with.

Bottom line, when you go to make a podcast you become a producer unless of course you work for a larger entity such as a radio network or station or a freelance producer who does it for you. It's all up to you, and no one else, to create the show each and every week. Part of being a producer is having a studio where you produce your show.

Think of your studio as a kitchen where you prepare your show. Like a kitchen you can choose to buy the highest priced appliances or go with the low level appliances. Both work the same when it comes to baking a cake and the same is true with a studio. You don't need an expensive kitchen to roast a turkey nor do you need an expansive studio to produce a podcast.

The following is a list of tools you will need to build your very own studio. I will show you the various levels of studios you can build to produce your show with, from the simplest to the most sophisticated. Keep in mind, when starting out people usually start with a minimalist studio and then move up to a pro studio as they grow their show and make money. The following are three versions of an in-home or in-office studio.

Real Simple Studio

- Lap Top Computer
- Audio Software
- Computer Microphone with 3.5mm jack that plugs into microphone jack on your computer
- Desktop microphone stand
- Headset
- Quite room

Pluses
Portability, low entry price, all in one system so there no need for external hardware other than microphone.

Minuses
Limited to a single mic, possible issues with poor recording quality due to lack of control over microphone volume which can most likely be fixed in the post-production phase using your audio software (added time in production).

In Between Studio

- Lap Top Computer
- Audio Software
- Two channel Mixer Board
- 2 higher quality microphones with standard microphone jack
- Microphone Cable
- Microphone stands
- Headsets
- Headset splitter jack which plugs into mixer which allows two headsets to be used at once
- Quite Room

Pluses

Portability, low entry price, small foot print, allows for two people at once, which opens up the show to having a guest or co-host.

Minuses

Limited to two microphones, higher cost of entry, bit more equipment to carry with you when doing remote shows, depending on mixer may not have built in compressor.

Pro Studio

- Computer
- Audio Software
- Multi-channel (4 microphone jacks or more) Mixer Board
- Pro quality Microphone
- Microphone Cables
- Microphone stands (table top or boom stands)
- Quality full ear protecting Headset (4)

- Microphone Extension cords and multi jack or microphone box (up to 4 microphone inputs) with separate volume level controls and single output cable that runs from mixer.
- Softphone hook up - Ability to bring in guests using a secondary computer equipped with a Soft Phone (Zoiper, Skype, etc.) which is routed out of the 3.5 mm speaker and microphone jacks to the mixer board.
- Misc. Cables
- Spit Shield/Microphone Cover
- Quite Room

Pluses

Allows for multiple hosts and guests, interfaces with remote guest/host via softphone system more flexibility. The built in compressor in mixer eliminates need to do it during the editing portion of your show production.

Minuses

No longer portable (will be a lot of work to carry to remote show locations), much higher cost of entry, more things to have to manage and learn in order to produce the show and more things to go wrong.

Creating a Quiet Room

It won't matter how much you spend on hardware if you don't have a quiet room to work in. A quite room does wonders to create a professional sounding podcast verses a poor sounding podcast.

Your job as a producer is to create a room where you eliminate as much echo and external background noises as possible. Keep in mind any background noise including echo due to a non padded room can be very distracting to listeners and may cause them to not listen to you.

You will need a quite room where you can do your recording in. I use my office space which I modified with acoustic ceiling tile, carpeted flooring, window shades, curtains and homemade baffling systems designed to deaden the room to eliminate echo. You will need to do the same with your room if you want the best quality.

Another thing you must contend with is ambient noise such as electronics, open windows, barking dogs and children in back ground.

In order to reduce ambient noise, you will need to turn off fans, electronic equipment (not used in the recording process), close doors and windows etc. to keep out outdoor noise. If you record your show at your home or apartment, choose a time when there isn't loud noises going on.

The first year I started producing the Hog Radio Show I used the third bedroom in our two story house which also doubled as my home office. We did pretty well, we even had guests show up to the house and come up stairs and do the show with us. The only drawback of having a home studio, were the occasions when my kids would open the door to peak in to see what we were doing. There was also the occasional crashes and noise they created in their bed room adjacent to the office.

I was able to get around this external noise by using quality microphones and compression technology which closes off the mic when it's not being spoken into. I was able to eliminate this ambient sound 95% of the time so it never came over into the show itself.

I must admit though, I have nothing but fond memories of those early days as a podcaster when my boys were a lot younger and still into what Dad was doing and wanted to be a part of it. I was even thinking of producing a show starring my sons where they would play music and talk about the stuff they enjoyed doing in between songs. Like many great ideas, I let that one slip through my fingers. A regret I still live with to this day.

The bottom line is this, do what you can to reduce the echo levels in your recording room and suppress external noise as much as possible. While I'm on the subject of children, if you have children at home do all you can to spend as much time with them, don't delay! Maybe you can create a show together. Before you know it, they will be graduating from High School and moving out of the house or they will grow too old to care any longer.

Time really does fly when you're raising kids. It seems like just yesterday I was starting my podcast. That was November 2007 and now it's 2016 and my sons are 8 years older. My middle son has entered college and my oldest son will be leaving as soon as he gets his financial stuff in order. My youngest is 13. Cool thing is he is working to become a You Tuber and is teaching himself how to use video editing tools.

Take it from a proud Father, do all you can to make time for your children because they won't be at home for much longer, soon will have an empty nest and the house will be silent. Relish the time you have with them while you have it.

Audio Software

The heart of your recording studio is your audio software. Audio software is what allows you to record the show and transform it into an MP3 File which is what you will need to create a podcast.

For full disclosure sake, I am only familiar with the audio software I use which is Adobe Audition 2.2. That said, most audio software works pretty much the same way. It allows you to record your show and edit it down to a radio ready or podcast ready MP3 File.

For those who will rent studio time then the studio will take care of the recording process for you. For those who use an online service such a Blog Talk Radio or Live 365 they will take care of it for you. Keep in mind there is a price attached to a studio.

Think about it this way, most radio personalities drive to a radio station and record their show there. The station furnishes an engineer who mans the mixer board, drops in the bumper music and even fields calls. He also records the show and gives you the final product after it has been aired over the air.

The very same thing takes place in a Television studio. People who work with TV studios rent production crews which typically are attached to station/studio. Once the show has been taped you will be given a copy of it.

This reminds me of my days as a rock and roller. My first band Tangent got ourselves onto a local Community Access Cable Station in Seattle where we performed ac 45 minute music set of our original music. We were given a VHS tape of our performance.

The point is most people can't afford to create a recording studio much less an in-house TV studio. It's far easier to rent studio time. In these cases, it makes sense to work with a producer like myself who can produce your show for you.

For those wishing to create their own studio, you should know there are two varieties of Audio Software: The paid variety and free variety known as freeware.

Freeware

You can locate free to cheap audio software programs by using the Web Browser Search Tool on your computer. Enter the term free audio software. Please note, there is Free and there is Trial Free. Trial free means you will not be able to produce an actual final copy without paying for the service. True freeware is just that, free.

Always make sure the software is compatible with your computer platform as in Windows or MAC. Both platforms have differing requirements and will need the right software. Make sure to read things over carefully before downloading anything.

In some cases you can also rent software but I prefer to purchase what I use knowing I can use it whenever and wherever I like. I prefer to own rather than lease but that's just me.

The plus side of freeware

It's free and it allows you a chance to experiment with creating audio files on your own, with minimal cost to you.

The negative side of freeware

The negative side is you will invest many hours in learning to use the software and once you get used to using it you may find out it doesn't meet your requirements. In this case you will have wasted time learning it and will need to relearn a more robust platform.

Paid ware

The adage you get what you pay for often is true so keep this in mind when you go to review the various paid for audio software packages.

The plus side of paid for

The audio software will be more robust and you will be able to grow into it rather than end up cursing it down the road.

The negative side of freeware

The number of choices can be daunting and each one will tell you they are the best. Some programs can be purchased outright, while others will only be offered on a monthly lease plan.

Audio Software Platforms

The best way to locate audio software is to use your internet search tool to search them out. Use the following terms when doing your search: audio software, recording software, audio software comparisons, free audio software, best verses worst recording software, etc. This will lead you to various forums and online sellers of audio software. The following is a list of both free and pay for audio software I am familiar with.

- Mixcraft by Acustica (This is what I'm using now)
- Adobe Audition
- Final Cut Pro
- SONAR by Cake Walk
- Zynewave Podium
- Virtual DJ
- Pro Tools
- Audacity
- Rose Garden

As I alluded to, each of these software programs have a steep learning curve attached to them which if you're tech savvy and used to working with software then you may pick it up quickly. If, on the other hand, you're like me and you're not technically savvy, then you may need to bring someone in to help you learn how to use the software.

Not being tech savvy myself I had to bring in a student from a local community college who was involved in their audio department. He came in as an intern engineer and operated the board for us for the first couple of months. (He received school credit for doing this). While he did this he was also instructing me on how to use the software on my own. By the end of his time with me, I was fully able to record the show on my own.

Another great resource for anyone wishing to get involved in podcasting or is currently involved in podcasting is You Tube. You Tube has many videos produced by professionals and novices alike devoted to helping you use recording equipment. Keep in mind the software they use will most likely be a different version than what you are running.

Updating Your Audio Driver

When uploading your Audio Software you may need to update your computers drivers. This will allow the software to operate properly on your computer. I suggest you do the following two things:

1. Go to www.driverupdate.com (Microsoft Approved) and purchase their Driver Update Software and download it onto your computer(s). This company requires you to speak to a customer rep when purchasing the software. Once you pay for the software they give you a download code which you use to download the software with. When you talk with sales rep they will work very hard to convince you that you need their monthly services. Don't buy it! Unless you're a mega company and need help. Just kindly decline and ask to pay for the Updater software and not the monthly maintenance service which runs over a $100.00 per month.

2. The second thing you may need to do is to update the ASIO driver on your computer. When I went to set up my Audition Software on my Laptop I had to activate the ASIO driver inside my computer via the Audition Software itself. Your software may require you to do the same thing. Note there are plenty of online forums these days that didn't exist back in 2006 so you will be ok.

   The following diagrams show you how to update the ASIO setting within Audition. Your software may be similar to Audition so I think it is worthwhile to explain what I am talking about.

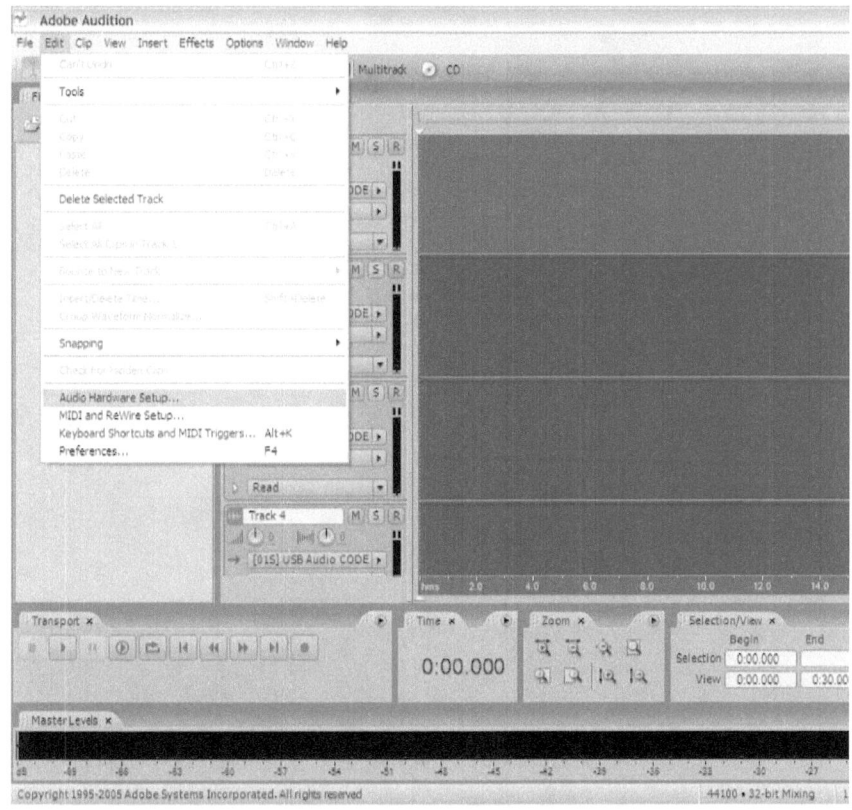

Chapter 7 Diagram 1 Updating your driver. When you open up your session screen you will need to click the edit button and scroll down to the Add Hardware and click the tab shown here.

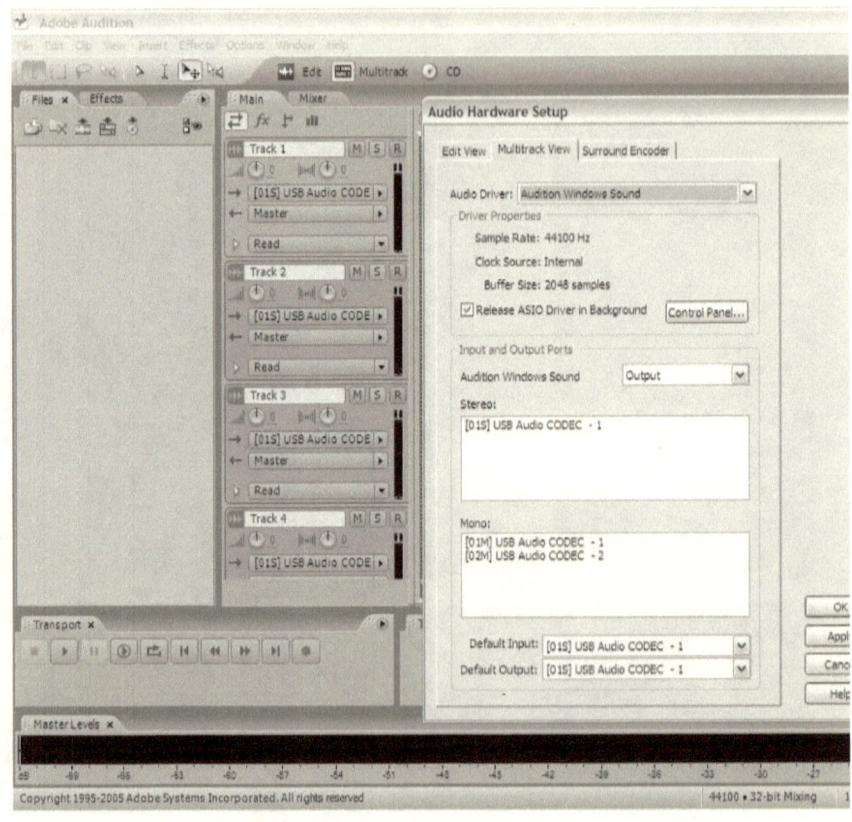

Chapter 7 Diagram 2 Updating your driver. The following window or something like it will open and you will see ASIO box. Place a check mark in it and click the APPLY button and save.

Keep in mind your software may be different and you may be able to skip this step in setting up your software. You might be able to pay a professional to set it up for you. A great place to find an expert is the local music store, who sells audio software. Be willing to pay for their time!

Using Your Equipment

Once you purchase the software and install it in your computer it's not going to do anything until you plug in your microphone at which point you will have a means of recording your voice into your audio software.

If you just use a computer without an external mixer all you need is a microphone and microphone stand made for a computer. You may wish to use a wind guard or a mic cover made from foam rubber but it's not necessary. I use an old nylon sock stretched over the mic to protect it from spit.

If you use a mixer board it will allow you to route more than a single microphone to your recording device. The following is a simple diagram of what my studio looks like showing how things are hooked up to each other.

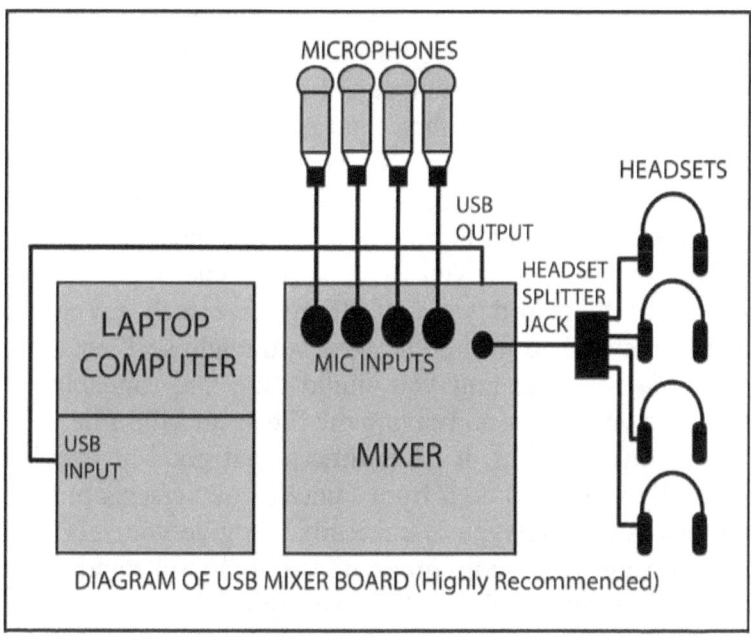

Chapter 7 Diagram 3 My personal Studio hardware.

The Diagram above shows my Stage III studio set up. I'm using a Behringer X1222USB mixer with built in compressor and effects unit which is plugged into my Laptop which contains my Adobe Audition Audio Software. The use of this mixer alleviates my need to route the microphones through a separate compressor then back into the computer, which I used to do in my Stage II Studio.

In all, I have gone through three studio set ups. The latest is very self-contained and gives me more flexibility to bring in more microphones should I have need to.

The plus side of using a mixer is it lets you have total control over the volume of each person using a microphone or input. You can, as I said above, run a cable from a secondary computer into the mixer allowing you to mix in more guests via soft phone interface. The cool thing about this type of set up is this allows you to record the conversation in real time and you sound just like a national talk show.

One more thing, if you want in-line compression you will need to add a compressor or buy a mixer with compression capability built in. Compressing your signal removes dramatic dips in the recording such as silent then loud noises, which make for a more even sounding recording. Note: many podcasters opt to add compression after the recoding and prior to creating an MP3 file. For me inline compression saves me time in post production.

The bottom line, you will need some type of recording equipment to record yourself. If you are tech savvy and have money to spend go for it, otherwise you might seek out someone in your area who can rent you studio time and can help you with recording your show and saving the file as an MP3 File,

One final thought, it takes time to get good at backing cakes especially when you do it from a cook book verses a pre-made in a box just add water type of cake mix. So give yourself time to get used to using your audio program, the audio tools and all the other steps that go into producing a finished product.

8
Pre-Production

Before you actually begin recording your show there are a number of things you should know that will help you work faster, smarter and produce a more professional sounding show. The following are some tricks of the trade I've learned over the years and, if applied, will give you a leg up over those who blindly go into podcasting. Keep in mind these tips are borrowed from the world of broadcasting, where I spent a bit of time.

In the world of producing there are three parts:

1. Pre-production.
2. Production.
3. Post Production.

These three parts go into producing a radio show, podcast, video, TV show, movie or a recorded song that makes its way onto the radio or your MP3 Player. Each of these media platforms have there own set of procedures they follow. For simplicity sake, I will only be focusing on the procedures used in creating a podcast.

This section deals with all the things you need to do before you actually click the record button and begin to talk into the microphone. Some of you may think, "Why do I need any steps" I know how to talk. That may be so but have you ever listened to someone ramble on incoherently for any length of time? It is pretty mind numbing and quickly gets tiresome.

In order for anyone who wishes to not be boorish but sound professional you would do well to incorporate these steps into your routine of creating a podcast.

Create an Outline of What You Will Be Talking About.

There is nothing more boring than someone who rambles on without much to say. In order to keep peoples attention you have to have a line of thought you are going down. A few shows of anything goes will quickly wear on the listener's ears and you will lose your audience. Even so-called out of controlled chaos heard on some shows is typically sketched out ahead of time so as to keep the show moving forward in a particular direction.

So write out a basic outline of topics you will cover and the amount of time allotted for each topic next to each topic. Have an order you will proceed down. If you're interviewing someone then create a list of questions you wish answered and use those questions as your outline. It's always a good idea to email the guest your questions ahead of the show date. This way they will be prepared and not caught off guard which can also make for a lousy show.

Example: Think of your show outline as giving a speech. You have an intro a middle and an ending. You also have various points you wish to cover along the way and you want to make sure you are catering to your audience's needs and best interests.

There isn't a professional talk show host who doesn't have a script. Even the people who sound wild and crazy have a script. They know in order to be lively and authentic they have to be well prepared and have a scrip to keep them focused for their entire show.

Next time you listen to your favorite show host see how they start the hour off and how they end it. You will quickly see they are following a logical line of thinking even if they get off topic they quickly get back on because they have a script.

Here is another example – watch your favorite TV Drama. Guess what, there isn't a word of dialog that comes from the actor's mouth that wasn't written for them to utter. Actors memorize their lines and then say them while being filmed. Actors do not go it alone, they follow a predetermined script, otherwise there would be nothing for them to say and the story would quickly evaporate.

If you're a solo show write down the amount I time you want to share each week and keep it to one of the following; 6 minutes, 15 minutes, 30 minutes or 60 minutes. Don't go beyond 60 as the average person is used to listening to 60 minute radio shows. Stay with what is proven and you won't go wrong. It's much better to leave people wanting more then to wear them out, with all your wonderful knowledge.

Writing Scripts/Outlines can a while to prepare depending on what you are doing. Keep in mind you're most likely doing the podcast to share insights with people you hope to have as a client one day. Make sure you do a very good job of sharing something people will appreciate. The goal is to have them think "Gee, that person really knows what they are talking about", "I can trust them to take care of me or buy their product".

Script Outline Example from the Hog Radio Show

> **Segment One.**
> *Welcome everyone to another hour of the best in Ridertainment; we've got a great show lined up for you.*
>
> Things seen out on the road/ News Report
>
> **- Break -**
> **Segment 2.**

Welcome back to the second segment of the Show.
This week's guest is _____

So we always start off with a few softball questions.

More questions…

- Break -

Segment 3.
Welcome back to the third segment of the Show.
(More Questions)

- Break -

Segment 4.
Welcome back to the fourth segment of the Show.
(More Questions)

- Break -

Segment 5.
Welcome back to the fifth and final segment of the Show.
(Show Wrap)

Chapter 8 Diagram 1 Show Outline. This is the style of outline we use each show. It allows us to stay on track.

Booking guests

If you're going to be a guest driven show or intermittently bring on a guest, you better set aside an hour or more a week to research and contact these potential guests. In my experience, I've used emails, cold calling and going through mutual acquaintances to find and contact potential guests.

Keep in mind your guests are busy people and may not have time right now so they may decline to be interviewed. Don't worry, because there are plenty of other people who enjoy sharing and they will gladly come on your show to be interviewed.

True story, when I first began producing The Hog Radio Show Motorcycle Podcast I didn't know anyone in the motorcycling world. I had to work hard to find people of interest to bring on my no name podcast. But that didn't deter me. I went online and began researching people who were somehow involved in motorcycling. It wasn't long before I was able to bring on a couple of legendary people from within the world of motorcycling. Once the first couple people came on, I was off to the races. Eight years later, I still bring some of those very same people back on the show.

The point is this, these people understood what it was like to chase a dream and they were willing to help me. I was chasing my dream of hosting a motorcycle podcast and they saw the value in what I was trying to accomplish. Nearly 400 guest appearances later I continue to work to find and invite new guests to come on the show.

Researching topics you will be covering in your show will also consume an hour or more a week of your time. I spend a minimum of an hour locating and copying news articles and press releases related to motorcycling. Depending on your type of show, you may spend a lot more.

In all likelihood, you would not be doing a podcast if you weren't an expert is something or have a passion for something you wish to share. That's passion is what causes you to spend time in preparation and outlining your show.

If you're an infomercial it will take longer to formulate your show. Part of running a company is spending time and money marketing it. So the time and money invested in creating your show, is just another facet of your overall marketing plan.

Speed up the process by doing a single take

To speed up the process of producing a podcast you can pre format your show and record it all in one take. This way you spend an hour in studio recording the show. There will be very little to do except a bit of post editing and uploading of the show to your Podcast feed.

I typically spend an hour recording each weeks show and another 5 to 10 minutes of post editing. There is the additional time it takes me to upload the show to the various online feeds. In my case, I record the show one day and edit and upload it on a different day.

Schedule your Time and Stick with It

When will you record the show? It's best to pick a certain day and time and stick with it. If you don't you'll always be struggling to juggle your time.

When we began we decided on Friday nights at 7PM PST which lasted for 8 years. In the winter of 2016 we switched to Wednesday nights 7PM PST. Keep in mind this is late for east coast guests but not too late as its 10PM their time and we've never had anyone turn us down for an interview (well okay a couple who go to bed by 7PM).

The point is this, whatever time you chose stick with it. This way you can schedule recording at the same time when booking guests. This has worked well for us and will work well for you.

Occasionally we attend a special event. In these cases we've set up our studio on location which is quite cumbersome but not impossible. For the past couple years, we've carried digital recorders with us to do the interviews. These portable devices, have given us more freedom to do interviews with people at these live events with the hassle of setting up our studio.

In those cases where we do portable recording, I end up with more on the back end editing these interviews down to fit into our pre-set shown times. It's well worth it to me as it removes the need to lug around our studio with us. We have had cases where we set up at an outdoor event only to have the wind blow over our microphone stands, which can be a costly.

Keep Your Mouth Shut

Keep your mouth shut when you have nothing to say. There is a myth that states you can have no dead air space so it needs to be consumed with your voice. Wrong, sometimes the best shows have plenty of pause space which works wonders to draw people in a little closer to hear what you have say.

It's better to say nothing than fill the time with ums and ahs and filler words. Stay quiet and move to the next topic in the show. Think of how you talk with a friend, you don't use ums instead you stay quiet until the next sentence or idea comes along.

At first you will be nervous and find yourself saying too many ums and ah's but that's part of the learning curve. The sooner you can wean yourself of the need to fill in blank spaces with non words the better. Keep in mind, it takes time to get good at podcasting so remind your-self of this and don't get flustered, just role with it.

Watch your Mouth

Keep it clean. I hate potty mouthed shows, they turn me off. Sure there is room for an occasional slip when someone is animated but how do the pros, do it? The real pros (not shock jocks and foul mouthed comedians) never cuss or use profane language and work hard to keep it clean. Can you talk without swearing? Sure you can. The cuteness of using foul language quickly wares off and you begin to sound like a hack (which in my opinion a lot of paid DJ's sound like). Anyone who has to swear throughout their show is lazy and doesn't have a good grasp of the English language.

For those of you who like to cuss and rant and swear a blue streak then have it but keep in mind a lot of people like myself will be turned off.

I know some of you are saying, dropping f bombs is all the rage today especially when producing a podcast. There is no FCC regulations stating you can't, so why not? "Look at those guys and gals on You Tube who cuss it up". True enough and so does Andrew Dice Clay and Tim Allen in their live shows. On the other hand Tim Allen doesn't use profane language in his TV shows. So even he can stick a sock in it when he has to or when he gets paid big bucks for doing so.

Bottom line, if swearing and potty mouth is what you want to do know that a number of providers will ask you to check a box that states you use profanity in your show. If you want to be the next Howard Stern then have at it. After all it's your life.

We live in a very jaded world where what used to be considered un-acceptable is now heard or seen in the media on a daily basis.

I would rather err on the side of PG maybe PG13 as I have self imposed standard for the way I carry myself and share my thoughts. I have children, parents a wife along with a reputation to uphold that has nothing to do with being filthy.

Be Dynamic But Be True to Your Self

When you begin you may be tempted to sound like your favorite talk show host hero. That's ok, many new hosts try to sound like someone they admire when first starting out. The sooner you can find your own voice the better. Your listeners want to listen to you, not a copy of someone else. People want authentic not fake.

If your comical then use comedy, if your serious then be serious, if your quiet (get louder) because you can't talk quietly in radio. You must be loud enough to make yourself heard. This doesn't mean you can't use a quite voice from time to time when making a point. Don't forget to use inflections; don't be monotone.

Creating Bumpers

A Bumper is what you hear at the beginning and ending of each show segment. Within each hour you have several breaks which include but are not limited to: News, weather, traffic, advertising and station ID. Podcasters don't have these breaks but you need breaks to run advertising (yours or sponsors). You may wish to have mini segments within your show. If this is the case you will need bumpers to announce each of these segments.

In brief a bumper is the musical/VO interlude that introduces the beginning or ending of these breaks. The following is a list of Bumpers.

- Show Introduction Bumper - Introduces your show for the first time.
- Exit Bumper - Signifies its time to go into a break.
- Intro Bumper - Reintroduces your show after the break.
- Show Exit Bumper - Signifies the show is over.

Keep in mind your podcast may never be aired on a radio station but there is still good reasons to add breaks into your show and with every break comes the need for a bumper to separate these breaks from the actual show segment.

Some show producers use music as a part of their intro and exits. Others just come right on as they are. If you wish to use music then you will be purchasing royalty free music from a music supplier. This is called Royalty Free Music but it's not free. You have to pay for the licensing fee which gives you the right to use the music without further charge.

Do you have friends who are musicians? If they have recordings they own and they are independent maybe they will let you use the music as a way to showcase their music. I have several bands that have given me permission to use their music at no charge.

Creating an opening bumper means recording the 10 to 30 second spot just as you would a regular show. Drop in the music and use the audio tools to edit the song into a short segment then you come back and add your voice or the voice of someone else who says (example) "Welcome to the Big John Show where we talk about the life and times of Robin Hood and his merry band of fellows". Then you edit the voice and music together, save file and then export the final product as an MP3 file.

Building bumpers will take time but it also means having fun as you learn to use your software to create short form intro's, exits and even ads for your self and possible clients. These files should be labeled and placed into folders on your computer that you can access later on when building your show template.

I won't show you how to create a bumper that's where your operating manual comes in. You can also get help from an outside expert or service provider.

Creating a Show Template

One of the slickest ways to produce a professional sounding show is to create a predetermined show template which includes all the elements found in a standard radio show.

The use of a template saves time and creates a Live Feel you don't get by just clicking record button and spending 60 minutes chatting. It will make your show sound just like the big guys on the radio.

The following diagrams will show you how I set up The Hog Radio Show template.

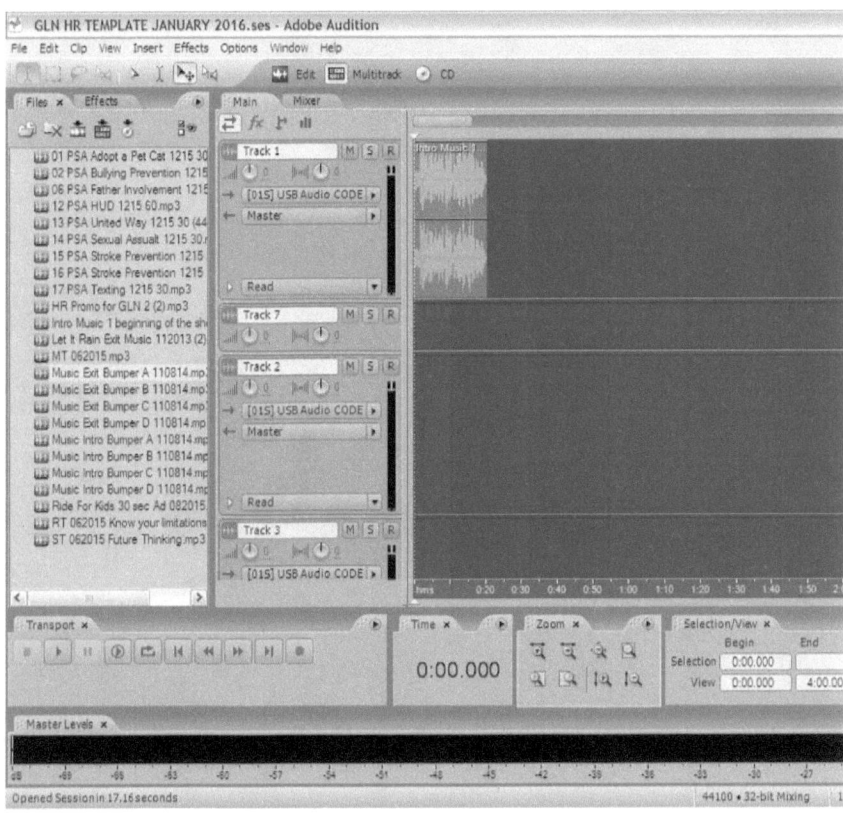

Chapter 8 Diagram 2 Show Template Creation. The picture you see is the intro bumper put into place.

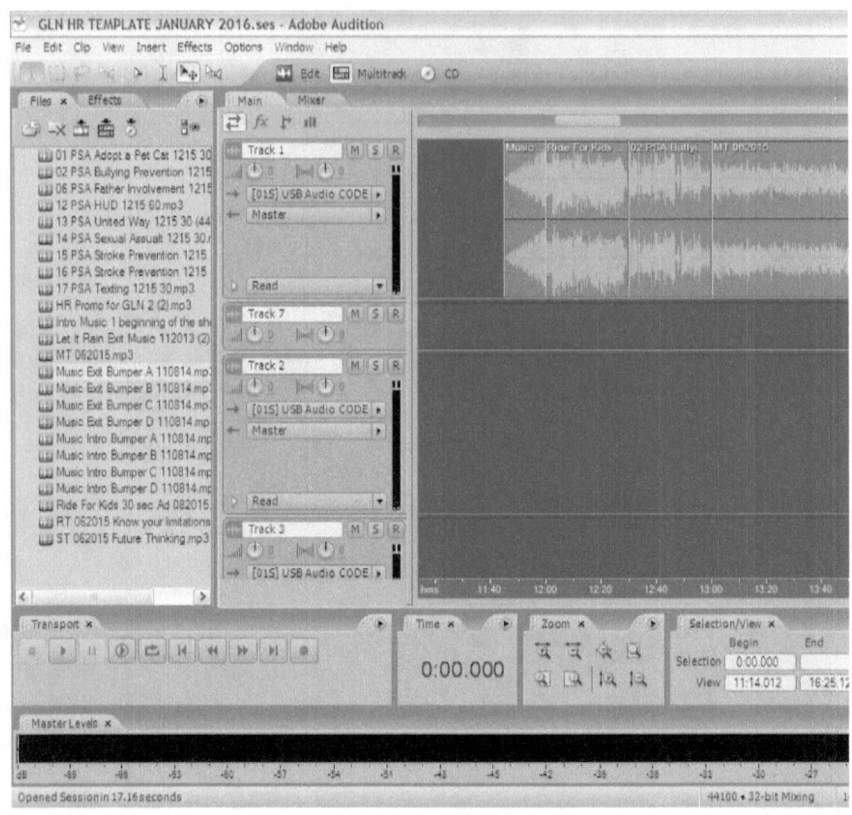

Chapter 8 Diagram 3 Show Template Creation. Here you see the first built-in break at 12 min mark which runs for a total of 4 minutes plus musical exit and intros that are added pre and post 12 and 15 min marks.

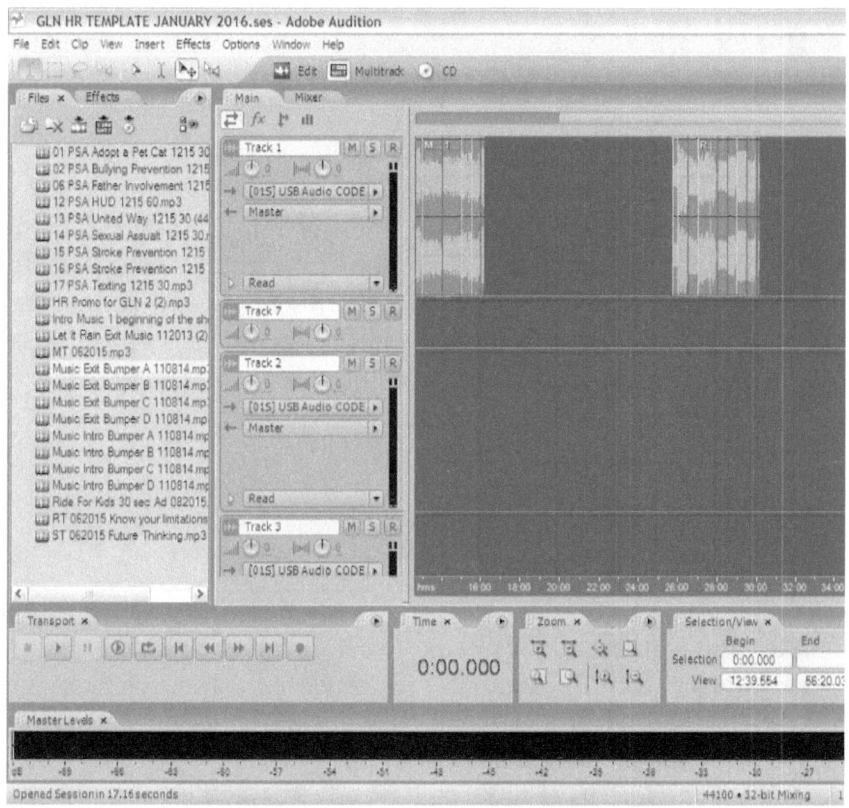

Chapter 8 Diagram 4 Show Template Creation. Here I have condensed the view so as to show you what the session template looks like. Each section is a 4 minute block of pre-recorded ads with a musical exit and intro added at both ends. The only exception is the last segment which is a 1 minute plus musical bumper.

For details on where to place the bumpers you can view Diagram 5 Station Clock in the following section. When I work with Radio Networks I have a given set of breaks they demand from me so I build my show around these predetermined breaks. In addition to their 3 minute breaks I add a 1 minute section to allow me a chance to sell ad space of my own. You may opt for a couple breaks and keep it simple.

Why I Use Bumpers

- Professionalism.
- Provides time to advertise (sponsors and yourself).
- Gives your show a "live feel". By having hard breaks you are often forced to stop midway into a interview or from sharing something. Then you are forced to come back from break and pick up where you left off, just like real radio!
- Having built in breaks forces you to stay within given a given set of parameters so you can't keep rambling on.
- Forces show into a predetermined format which saves you time and keeps you on track.

Creating a Show Clock

All radio stations have a Radio Clock inside their studio and their networks as do TV stations and networks. These clocks signify when a local ad or a national ad will be interjected into the hour time slot you are on the air.

TV and radio have to be paid by advertising they sell, otherwise there would be very few TV shows or radio show to watch or listen to. Since there are ads to be aired, the networks or stations build in certain amounts of time each and every hour where they run their sponsors ads. If you want to have your Podcast aired on a radio station it's a good idea to get used to a radio clock.

The Hog Radio show is based on a radio clock that we run off of. It was given to us by a station we were airing on years ago. We continue to use the same clock so we can air our show on any given station/network should we chose to do so.

These breaks provide us with time within our show we can offer to sponsors who wish to reach our audience. In the beginning, and even to this day, we run Public Service Announcements in the places we have no paid advertisers.

It will go something like this:

1. Create the original show template as explained above – using the bumpers you created along with Sponsor supplied Ads or PSA. Once the show template is created you save it naming it (Your show name here with date). Once the show template is saved you can use it anytime you go to create a show.
2. Open the show Template (under Open Session) find the show template and open it up.
3. Once the template is open, click the Save As and name it the new show Episode title.
4. Record using the template.
5. Save the show and then Export the show as an MP3 File under the same title you named that episode.
6. When Exporting is complete Close Out of the recording session and close down the audio software.
7. Repeat process every time you go to do a show. When replacing ads once completed save and you have an updated Template.

When you build a show template it's a very good idea to use your show clock to make sure all the times align correctly. The following is a diagram of my show clock I created using Excel. The times coordinate with the Radio networks clock. Note, the time you will see in your audio software begins at 00.00 and then moves forward. This allows you to create breaks exactly where you want them to be within your show. The finished show will align with radio clock or your own studio clock.

Hog Radio Show PROGRAM CLOCK

Seg	HR Clock		Description
	00:00		*First Segment*
3 min	**12:00**		Network Commercial Break (3 min)
	15:00		*Second Segment*
	16:00		.60 sec HR Commercial Time
3 min	**26:00**		Network Commercial Break (3 min)
	29:00		*Third Segment*
	30:00		.60 sec HR Commercial Time
3 min	**41:00**		Network Commercial Break (3 min)
	44:00		*Fourth Segment*
	45:00		.60 sec HR Commercial Time
1 min	**53:00**		.60 sec HR Commercial Time
	54:00		*Fifth Segment*
	55:50		Station Break (Station ID)
			Top Of the Hour

Chapter 8 Diagram 5 Radio Clock. This diagram shows how I use Excel to create a show clock that mirrors the radio station/network clock. It shows the exact times where I need to build breaks and add bumpers.

9

Production
Recording the Show

In the last chapter, we looked at what it takes to create a show template but I didn't go over setting up your software so you can create a show template or a bumper, for the matter. So in this chapter I go over setting up your recording software to create a professional sounding recording.

When creating a recording there are numerous settings you can use. Some producers are able to create high quality sounding MP3 Files using low fidelity settings for their original recording. These types of low fidelity recordings are used when creating bumpers and ad spots. Other producers like myself, prefer to create all our recordings using high fidelity settings.

What I will be showing you is what I call the middle of the road approach which works great for a talk show. Unlike music a talk format doesn't require as high a fidelity setting. Keep in mind, the higher the settings the greater the memory required.

Most podcast services can't accept a file above 100MB and prefer sizes to be below 50MB for an hour show. By following my example you can find a happy medium which takes less memory.

Insider Tip - I used to save my MP3 Files in Stereo until I worked with a radio network who asked me to save the MP3 in Mono (while keeping all the other settings the same). I ended up reducing the size of my final podcast ready MP3 File substantially.

What used to be a 50MB File is now 38MB.

The following are the steps I use to create the setting used when making a recording. The original recording session should always be created in a WAV file. The session as it's called will be saved in the WAV form. (see your manual for details). When you're done recording the show you should always save it. Then while it still open you use the Export tab and save it as a MP3 File.

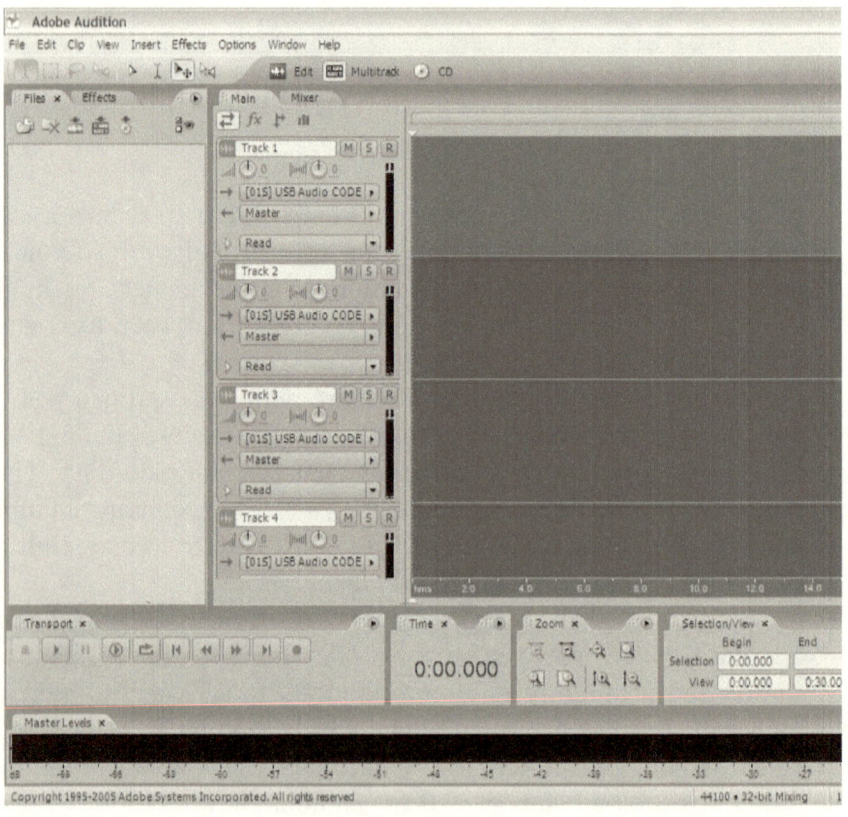

Chapter 9 Diagram 1 Recording Session. When you open your recording session it should look something like this.

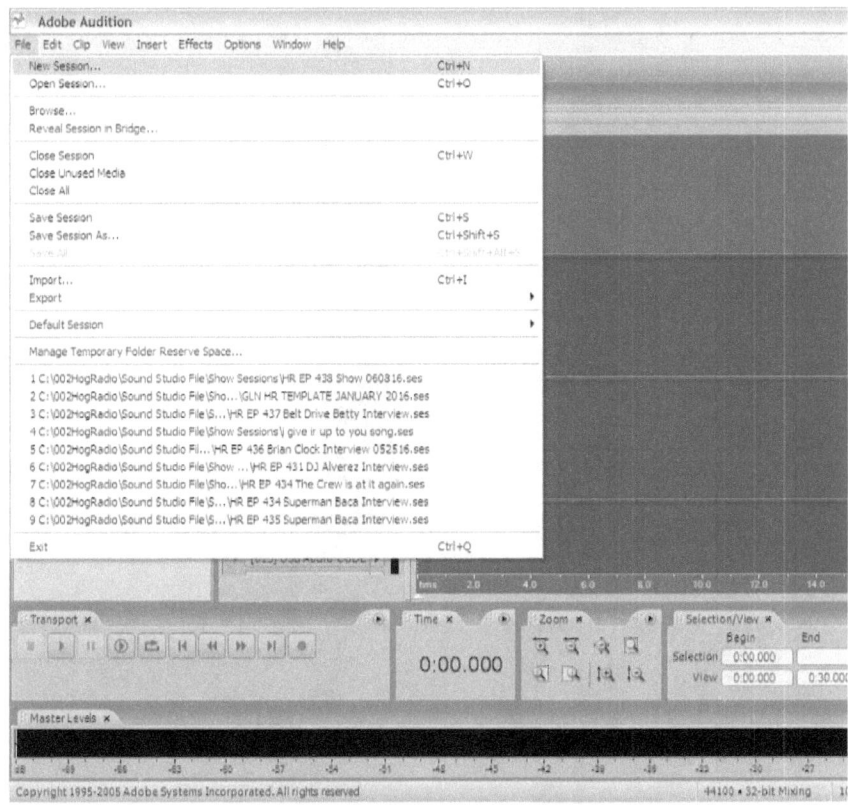

Chapter 9 Diagram 3 Recording Session. In this window Click the File Tab at the top left. When the new window opens up when it does highlight the New Session Tab and click it (as shown here).

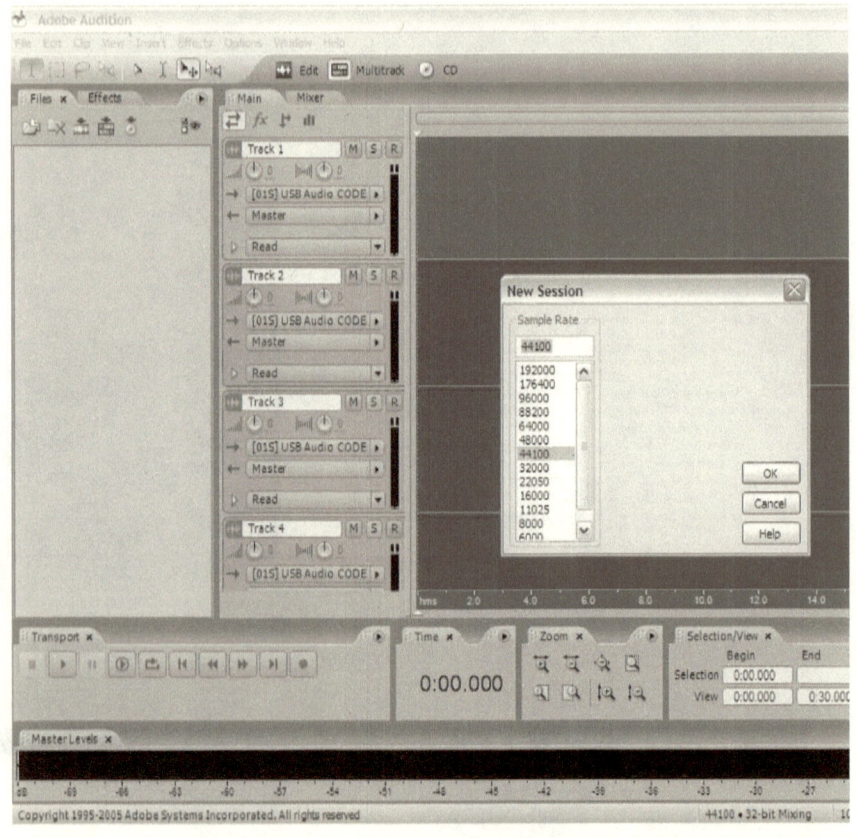

Chapter 9 Diagram 3 Recording Session. This is the next window you will see. Use the arrow and scroll down till you see the 44.100HZ value as shown here. Highlight the value then click the OK tab (as shown here).

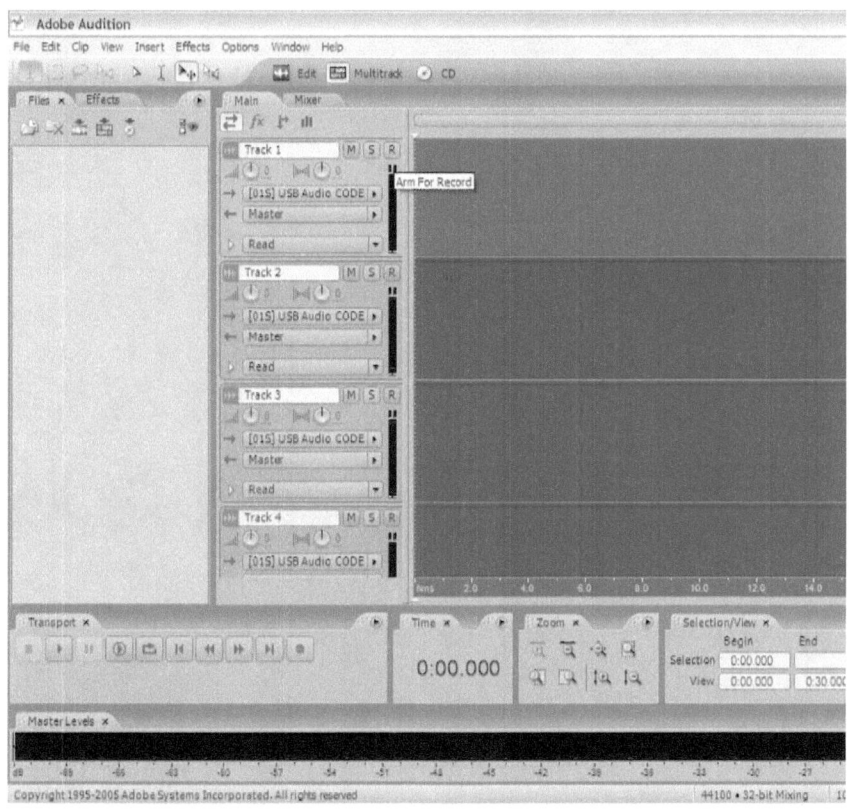

Chapter 9 Diagram 4 Recording Session. Once you have clicked the settings this window will appear as show in this picture. You will see a Green, Yellow and Red button at the left or wherever your software places it next to the track you will record with. In this window you'll see several tracks each with their associated buttons. Click the Red Button in the Track you choose to record in. When you do the next window will pop up and look something like the following diagram.

Chapter 9 Diagram 5 Recording Session. Here is where you name the session (original recording session created in a Wav file). Once you name it and save it to a safe place on your computer you will be getting ready for recording. (Note, I have numerous places all organized on my computer for each audio recording/file you will need to do the same). Once you do this, the next window will appear as shown in the following diagram.

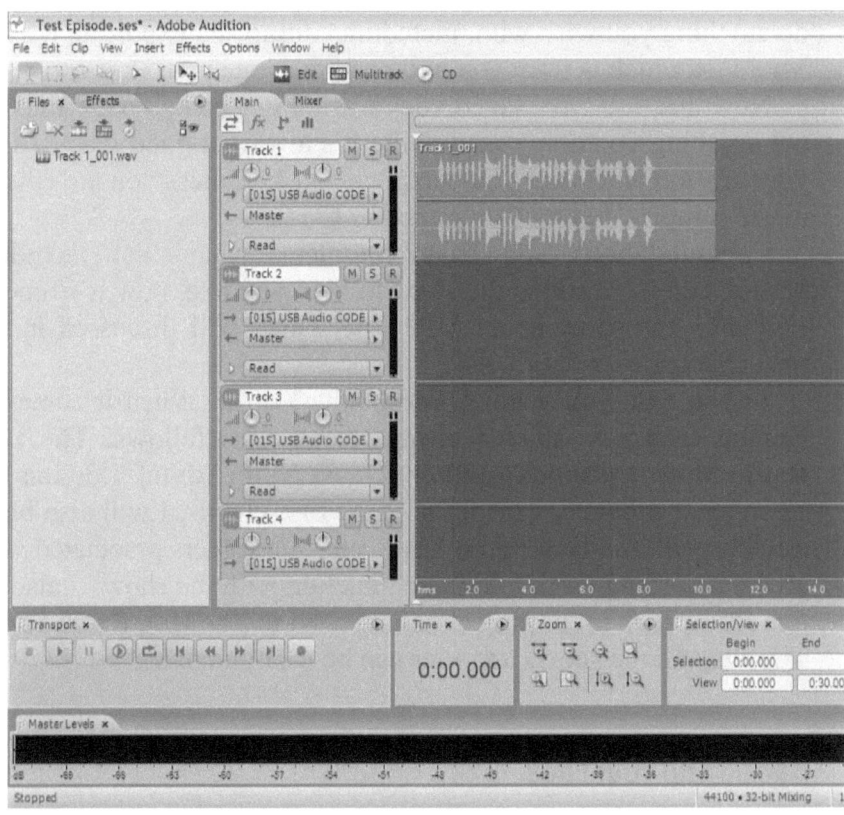

Chapter 9 Diagram 6 Recording Session. It's time to record. Now that you have created a session name you are ready to record. In order to record you will need to leave the red tab clicked in track 1 as shown here (or whatever track you work with). Now you must click the Big Red Tab at the bottom left (my audio gear, yours may be different) which activates the recorder and allows you to begin recording your voice.

PLEASE NOTE, YOUR SOFTWARE MANUAL WILL WALK YOU THROUGH THE RECORDING PROCESSES.

Once you have completed your recording session it's time to save it. All you need to do is click the File Tab upper left scroll down and click the Save Session tab and you have an audio file you can do anything you wish with, including editing and exporting it as an MP3 File which is what you will need to create your Podcast.

Now that you have saved your session you can go back and edit out anything you don't want. Note it's always a good idea to save your session whenever you complete a task (Unless you are editing music samples, but that's for another time).

Congratulations you have completed your first recording session and have edited the show to how you like, now it's time to EXPORT the show as an MP3 File which will discussed in the next chapter.

Just in case you want to know how I do it. When it comes to naming each new show I always name it as follows: **The Hog Radio Show Episode (number) Guest Name (date)**. I do this for all shows I produce, whether its mine or a clients. I will also build a folder with the Hog Radio Name and sub folders associated with all the recording work I do in conjunction with the show. I also do this for each client or project not attached to The Hog Radio Show. This way all the shows and files can be easily found.

Backing up Your Files

Backing up your computer or individual files is something many people get too busy to do then regret not doing when their computer crashes. When it comes to saving audio files you must back them up. The following are ways I back up my audio and all the other files.

1. CDROM. This was my preferred way of backing up MP3Files in the early days.
2. Flash Drive. This has become my go-to method of backing up all my files and recording sessions.
3. External Hard Drive. I have begun backing up all my audio files using an external hard drive in addition to flash drives. Double insurance is cheap insurance.

There are Two Types of Audio Files to Save

1. WAV Files. This file is the original recording session file you save when you're done recording the show. These files are a WAVE File. Wave files are your primary recording and editing files. They are the purest audio file you can work with so it's important you save these files in case you need to go back and edit them later. Think of what used to be known as a negative for your camera film. You make prints off of a negative. Well it's the same for audio in that you make MP3 Files off of WAVE files.

   Another reason is Wav files are huge and you will need to back them up and then eventually remove them from your computer. I save the last 5 sessions and delete the rest after I have exported it to an MP3 File (with the exception of my original show template and associated wav/mp3 Files, which always stay on my computer).

2. MP3 Files. These are the files you will need to upload to your Podcast Service provider. These files also can be played on an MP3 Player. MP3 Files are made by using the Export Tab under the file tab which will be dealt with in the next session.

   MP3 Files will also need to be backed up and eventually deleted from your computer as they also take up room. By using the settings described in the previous chapter and the ones in the next chapter you will get high quality recordings without using as much memory.

When I began saving my files I would save them at a very high fidelity level making each hour long MP3 File 100 MB. Two things happened when I did this:
1. The files ended up being to large for the service provider I used and would play very slow.

2. They became large and took up lots of memory on my hosting site and within my laptop.

To overcome this problem, I broke my show into two parts which worked for a short time. Figuring there should be a better way I re-read my manual and discovered I could reset my recoding setting including the MP3 exporting settings. I ended up with a 60 minute show coming in at 50MB. This enabled me to upload podcast as a single show. Today my 55:50 minute show is saved as a single high quality 38MB MP3 File.

Reasons to Back up Your Audio Files

- Prevent loss of files if your computer crashes.
- To free up memory. Audio files hog your memory so they need to be backed up to a secondary memory device then deleted from your computer.

There are 2 types of files you'll primarily be working with: The WAV file used in creating your original recording session. The MP3 File used in creating a podcast. The following chapter explains how to create an MP3 File from a WAV file.

10

Creating an MP3 Audio File

When it comes to making a podcast you need an audio file that is conducive to being played through the podcast feeder service provider. The only type of audio file accepted by podcast services is the MP3 file format. When you purchase a song from iTunes or another online portal what do you get? Yep, an MP3 File which is housed on your IPod, mobile device or in your computer to be played on its internal MP3 Player.

Creating a podcast has many steps. The following is a list of these steps.

1. Launch your template (if you use a template)
2. Record the show
3. Save the show as a session (WAV file)
4. Export the show as an MP3 File
5. Upload the MP3 File to your podcast service provider(s)

In this section I will show you a step by step process to transform your high quality recording session into a high quality MP3 File that meets the requirements of today's popular podcast service providers. The following is a step by step guide for creating an MP3 File.

Using Export Tab to Create MP3 File

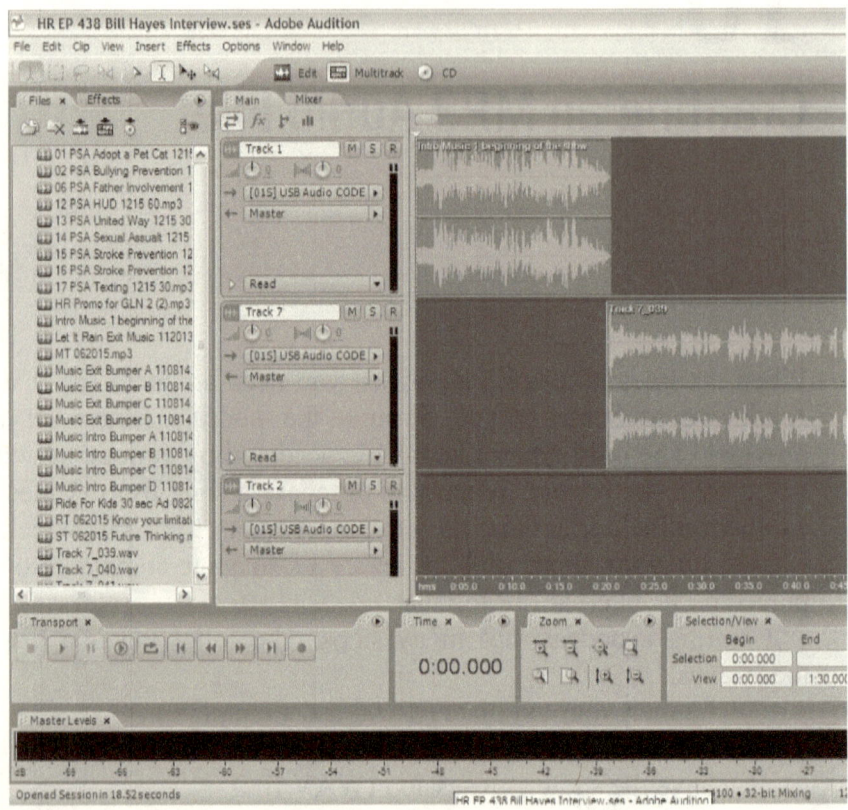

Chapter 10 Diagram 1 Creating an MP3 File. This window shows a fully recoded and edited and saved session ready to be Exported.

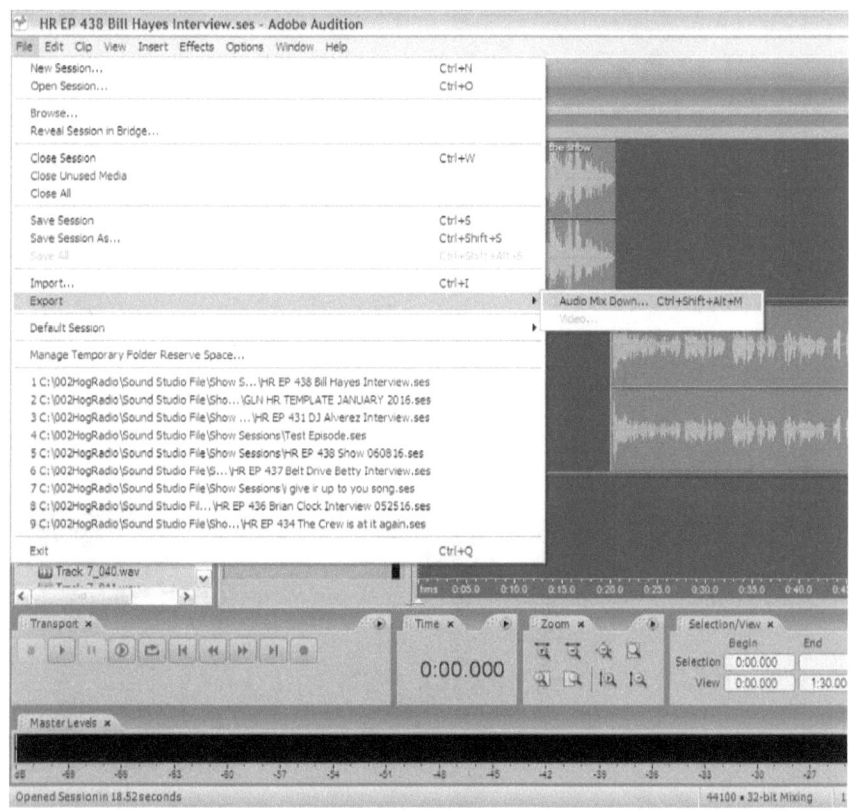

Chapter 10 Diagram 2 Creating an MP3 File. Click the File Tab as shown, highlight Export tab then click the Audio Mix Down Tab (shown here in Gray).

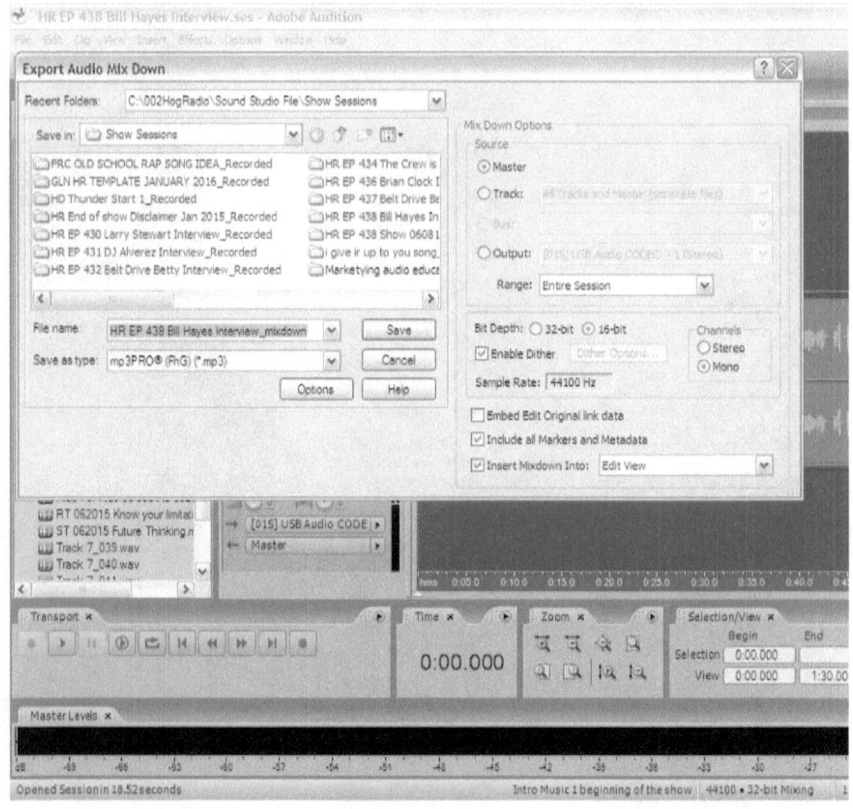

Chapter 10 Diagram 3 Creating an MP3 File. Once you have clicked the Audio Mix Tab this window will open revealing the File Name Box and the Save as type Box along with several other options. Duplicate as much as possible the settings you see in this window. Then Click Save tab for a new box.

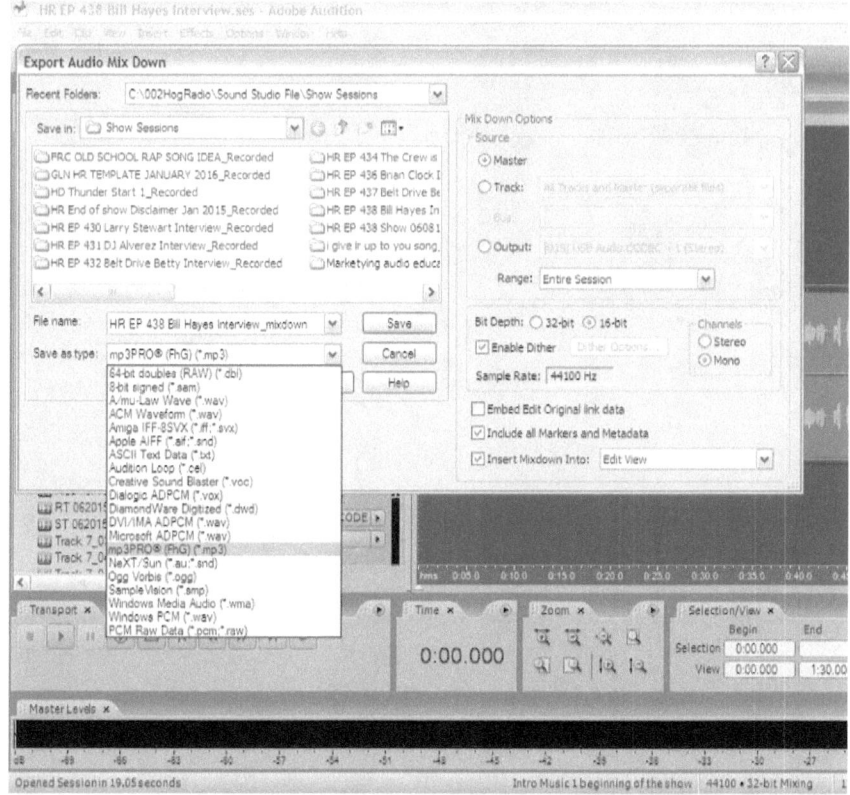

Chapter 10 Diagram 4 Creating an MP3 File. This is the window will appear next. Scroll down the list, highlight the MP3 Pro and click on it. Once you do this it will take you back to the window shown in Diagram 3. Once you are back to what Figure 3 looks like click the Options tab.

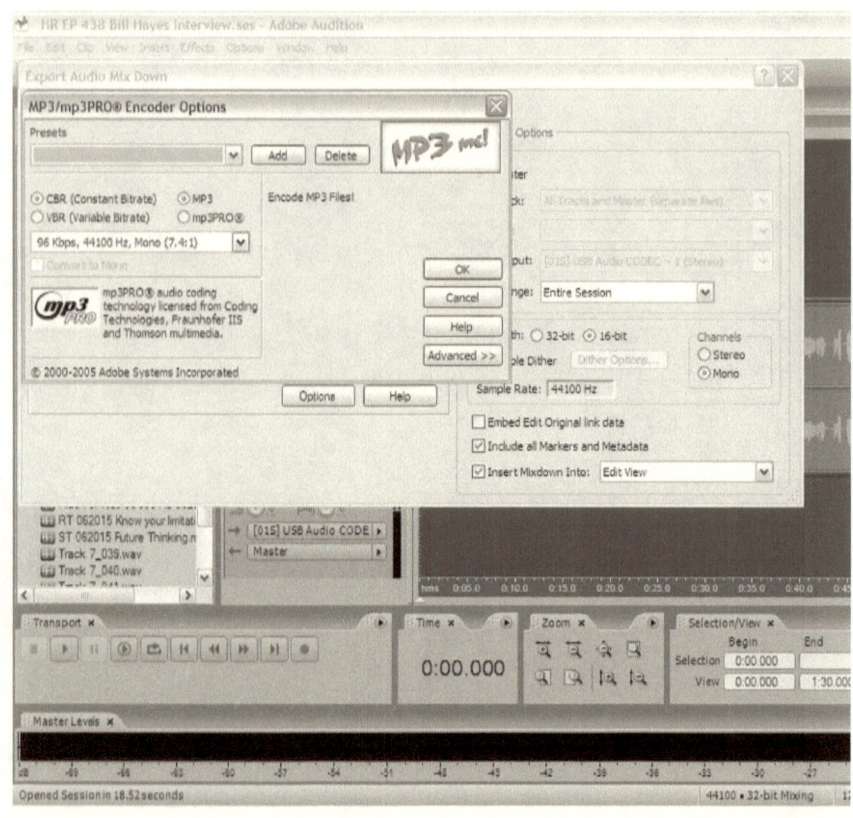

Chapter 10 Diagram 5 Creating an MP3 File. The next window that opens will look like this. In left hand box as shown here (or where-ever your box is located) click the arrow and locate this setting from among your list of settings. Now set your MP3 File Settings to what is shown: 96db/44.1000HZ then click the OK tab which will return you to the previous window. See next Diagram.

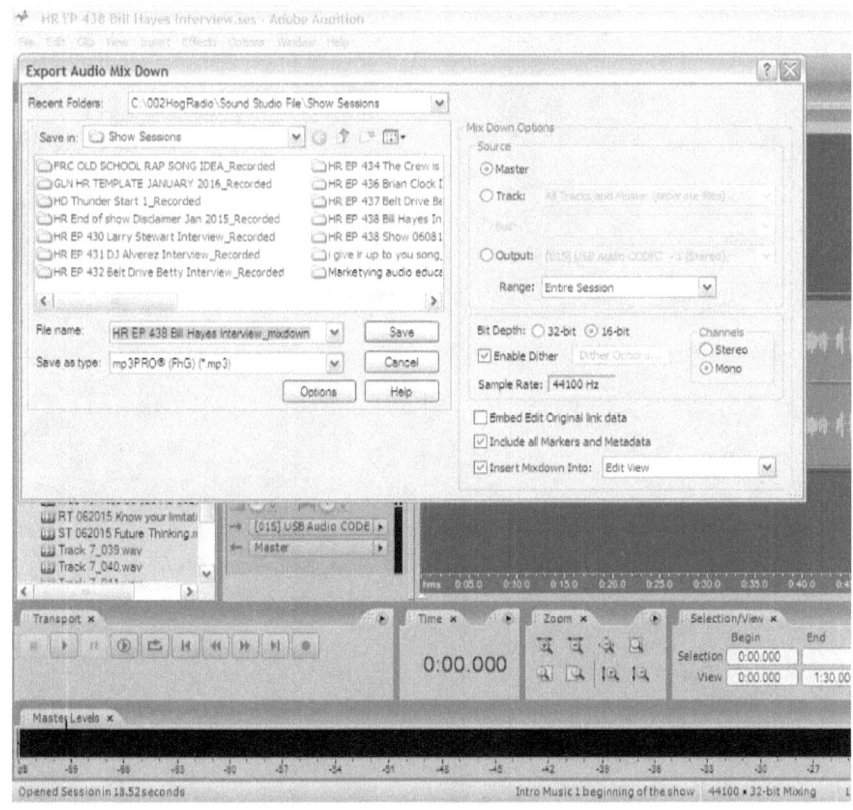

Chapter 10 Diagram 6 Creating an MP3 File. Once you're back in this window click the Save Tab which will create a mini window shown in next diagram.

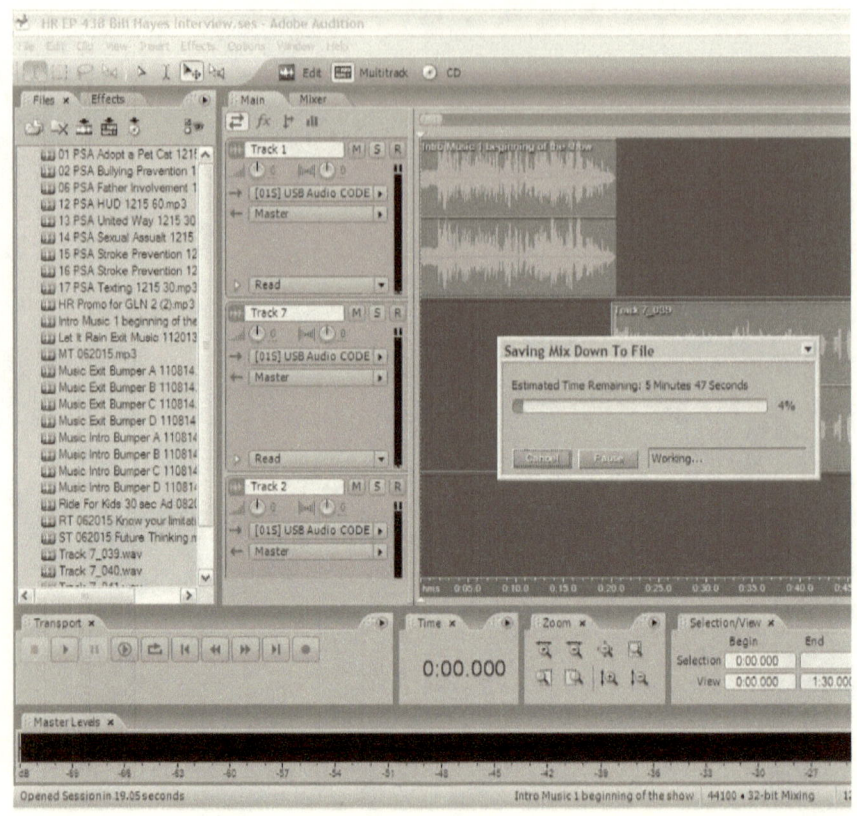

Chapter 10 Diagram 7 Creating an MP3 File. This is the final step to creating your MP3 File. This step usually takes several minutes so relax and do something else, while the software is doing its thing.

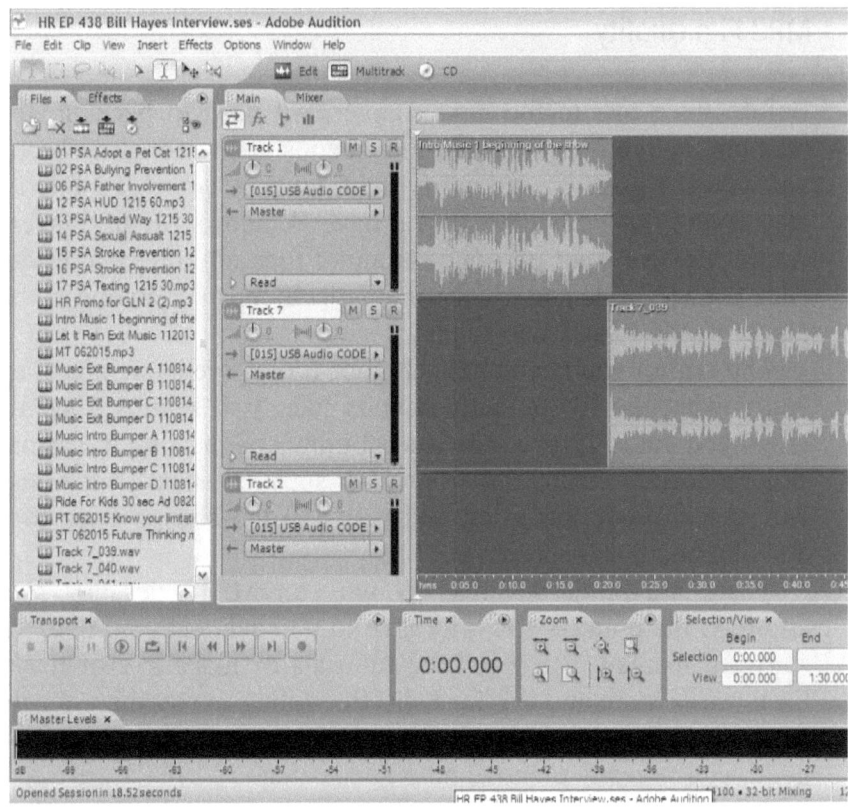

Chapter 10 Diagram 8 Creating an MP3 File. Once the file is done saving, it will return to the recording session window shown here. At this point, you can close out and move onto the uploading phase.

Please note, your software will function differently than what I am showing you in these diagrams. The point is to use the settings as instructed so you get the best quality from your MP3 file without using up too much memory. By holding to these setting as much as possible you will save yourself time and come out with a professional sounding Podcast.

In the following chapter I will cover the basics of transforming your MP3 File into an actual Podcast.

MP3 File Quality

Before we move to the next chapter, we need to back up for a moment and verify your MP3 File sounds good enough to become a podcast. A great way to verify the fidelity of your MP3 File is to play it on your computer. If you have Windows Media Player or Apple Media Player on your computer then all you have to do is click the MP3 File and it will automatically open up in one of these player windows and start to play.

The reason you need to check your file before launching it is to verify what the file actually sounds like. If it sounds good then bravo you got it. If it sounds kind of tinny and metallic or has other strange sounds emanating from your speakers, then something is wrong with your recording and you will need to go back to the drawing board and sort it out.

There are numerous reasons why an MP3 File may sound crummy, the point is you will have to go back and read over your software manual, use YouTube tutorials or make a visit to your local music store and ask for help. Be willing to pay them for their help. Once you have this ironed out and your MP3 File sounds good, you're ready to move onto podcasting.

11

Publishing your Podcast

Now that you have an MP3 File you're going to want, to make it available to as many people as possible. In this chapter I will run through the two methods to make your podcasts available to the public. In the world of podcasting there are two methods to make your show available:

1. Host your podcast on your own website.
2. Have your podcast hosted by a podcast hosting site.

Both methods have their positives and negatives. In this chapter we will cover the following two methods. For those hosting their own podcast on their website you will need to use what is called a podcast plugin. For those hosting their podcast on a second party hosting service, make sure they offer the ability to get your feed to iTunes and other major directories.

Before we go onto the two methods of podcasting I wish to clarify something regarding your website. Websites vary in the way they are built. For the purposes of this section, I will be talking about what I'm familiar with which is WORDPRESS. This is what I use for The Hog Radio Show website. That said what I share below should still be applicable to your situation no matter what type of website platform you use.

A Quick Word about WORDPRESS

WORDPRESS is one of the most popular platforms used to build websites with today. Hence there are more plugins built that can be incorporated into the WORDPRESS platform than any other platform that I know of. Included in this list of plugins are podcasting plugins which can be incorporated right into your website.

Note, If your website platform is built off of other technology don't worry, there are plenty of podcast plugin providers you can work with.

What you need to host your Podcast on your own website. The power of Plugins

When looking at the various Plugins you can use to podcast with through your website you should know all are not equal in what they offer in way of features. Do your homework, before you go with a particular plugin. The following is a short list of things to look for in a plugin. Oh and some of these plugins offer free tracking while others charge a small monthly fee.

Having learned the hard way, you will do well if you choose a plugin that allows you to do the following things:

1. Upload your feed to as many directories as possible including ITunes and Stitcher.
2. Let you track the number of listens/downloads per each episode.
3. Play on any website/media platform without having need for the listener to turn off their Ad Blocker before listening/downloading the show.
4. Tracking where the listener is coming from such as iTunes or organic (directly from our website).

5. Tracking must be accurate as in only listens and downloads not visits to the website.
6. Is it free or do you have to pay for tracking. Will they give you a free trial period before signing up? Ask the Customer Support people before you download or pay for plugin.

The following is a non-exhaustive list of 7 popular podcast plugin providers that work with WORDPRESS. Note, when you visit these provider websites make sure to see if they also work with other platforms should you have another website platform you are working with.

Seven Plugins that work with WORDPRESS

- Seriously Simple Podcasting
- Blubrry Powerpress
- Smart Podcast Player
- Podlove
- Cincopa
- Podcasting Plugin by TSG
- Libsyn Podcast Plugin

Podcast Hosting Websites

Let's say at this time you don't want to house all your shows on your own website and would prefer an alternative way to get your podcasts to people. No problem, there are several options for doing this.

When it comes to podcast services there are two options: Paid hosting and non-paid hosting. Paid hosting service providers offer a number of things such as archiving of past shows, tracking services and promoting your podcast within their podcast directory. Many of these very same services also provide a free but limited version.

Non paid hosting services offer limited archiving, very limited to no tracking and no internal promotions. Some will allow you to use their platform to get your podcast listed on iTunes and other directories. Some hosting services host thousands of podcasts while other host, hundreds. So do your homework.

The following is a list of podcast hosting services you will want to check out.

- Podomatic
- Podbean
- Libsyn
- Blogtalkradio
- Soundcloud
- Buzzsprout

Mobile Podcast Applications

Mobile applications allow listeners the ability to download your podcast to their mobile device. These applications can be accessed via your podcast plugin or separately. Make sure the plugin/hosting service you choose lets you create a feed link between your plugin/host and Stitcher and iTunes.

- Sticher - used for Android based phones.
- iTunes – used for iPhones

For full disclosure, I started out using a Godaddy product which they discontinued. In my need to jump into a brand new website and not lose my podcasts (I had a 30 days time to transfer 350 shows onto a new platform). I had my webmaster design a new website then find a plugin that would let me podcast from my new website.

Unfortunately due to our lack of understanding of podcasting plugins at the time she chose a less than optimal plugin (not listed above). I was desperate to get things up and running as quickly as possible and should have done more homework on my own. Hindsight is better than foresight.

I currently use the plugin and Podomatic to get my feed onto iTunes and other directories.

My goal is to switch over to the Blubrry Powerpress Plugin.

Note, some of the plugins allow you to migrate your show feeds from one platform to your new one. When doing this it will often require you to change the RSS Feed address which can cause problems with Apple iTunes no longer accepting your show. To remedy this challenge I will keep the old plugin in place for the archived shows and add the new plugin for all new shows moving forward. Having lost all my connectivity once before, I am not taking any chances on that happening again. One thing I have learned is it's better to be safe than sorry.

Hopefully you have enough information now to get your MP3 File into a podcast form and available for listening via a podcast platform.

There are numerous steps to creating a show and making it available to the public. It's certainly not for the faint of heart. That said, it's very doable, if you have a plan of action. Getting your show hosted is just the beginning. You also have to promote the show, otherwise no one knows its there.

The following chapter will give you some tips to grow your audience.

12

Ways to Grow Your Audience

In my Twelve Myths to Podcasting Report I explained just because you launch a podcast you better not expect to become an overnight success. What you will need to do to grow your audience is to work just as hard to market your podcast as you do to produce it. The following are ways to do this.

Leverage Your Guests

If at all possible have the guests you bring on the show agree to promote the interview they did with you by placing a direct link of the podcast interview on their Website, Blog, Email, Facebook page and any other social media outlets they may use. They can also send out Press Releases and Tweets telling their followers to listen to the interview.

Most guests love to promote themselves and there isn't a better way than for them to place a link of the interview you did with them on their website.

Some guest are so savvy they will tweet out ahead of time that they will be appearing on your show and then tweet again once they have loaded the show to their website. The point is to have your guests promote your podcast through their online outlets.

- Facebook Page Post (the show will show up on their page)
- Website under the News/Media section

- Twitter (you need to give them your twitter tag attached to your website/link of the post
- Newsletter
- E-Blast
- Other online outlets they may use
- E-Press Release

Leverage All Your Social Media Network Connections

It's up to you to leverage your social media outlets to promote the show.

- Linked In
- Facebook
- Twitter
- Instagram
- Email
- E-Press Releases

Make sure to place links of the show (where possible) into each of these outfacing distribution systems shown above. Think of these outposts you very own PR service where you distribute your content. Depending on the website and player you chose you will be able to automatically upload the show to your Facebook and other online outposts through one portal.

Create internal Self Promo's

One of the easiest ways to self promote is through in show promotions that are designed to drive people to your website and sign up for your free newsletter. You can do this as part of your show or as part of your ads (if you have built in advertising breaks). Even if your show is only housed on your website the goal will be to get it placed onto as many podcast directories as possible.

Getting Listed on Podcast Directories

One of the major ways to expand your audience is to get your show listed on as many networks as possible. Network is another name for Directory. A directory is where thousands of shows are hosted and made available to subscribers to listen to or download.

Most people have heard of iTunes but they're just one Directory (hosting service) there are countless others. To be honest, this can be a bit confusing. Even as I try to use the proper descriptions, I get confused. Why these providers didn't use the same descriptions found in traditional media is beyond me.

You may have to link your shows feed via your plugin housed on your website. This is why it's important to work with a Plugin provider that offers you the most feed options as possible. The following, is a list of directories you will want to look into and possibly get your show uploaded to.

- iTunes,
- Stitcher
- BluBrry
- Google Music Cast
- Microsoft Music
- Blog Talk Radio
- Pod Bean
- Sound Cloud

These Online and Mobile Application outlets make your show available to millions of prospective listeners and are powerful "NETWORKS" to get your podcast heard on. But you will still need to market your show as there are thousands of shows to choose from and yours may get lost.

Business cards, flyers and other traditional outlets

Handing out business cards and flyers is an excellent way to get the word out about your podcast. You can hand them out at tradeshows and your social gatherings. You can include a custom magnetic code which allows recipients with smart phone to go directly to your website bypassing the need to type in your website address.

Traditional Broadcasting

Another way is to go outside the podcast world into the Broadcast world. An example of this is Adam Carolla who has partnered with 30 year Broadcasting veteran Dennis Prager. Adam befriended Dennis and they got along well enough that Dennis brings Adam on his show several times a year which is another opportunity to promote his website and podcasts to millions of listeners. They've even done live shows with each other in various locales across the country.

Newsletters

Build your own mailing list by creating a companion newsletter which people get when they sign up for it. This allows you to send out reminder e-blasts of upcoming or past shows.

No matter how you go about building an audience it takes time. If you're not careful it can become a full time job, so understand this going into it. There is no such thing as an overnight success. It takes lots of time, tenacity and money to create a sizable audience.

Events

Attend events. Use your cards and hand them out to people you meet at various events you attend. In the early days of podcasting we worked to set up our show booth and do live interviews then I would walk around handing out dozens of cards and in some instances hundreds of cards. This helped us grow the show in the early days.

Contests

Use contests to capture emails and grow your audience. You can create give away items, such as stickers, posters, prizes you get from participating sponsors or books by authors you interview.

Contests have long been used by Radio Stations to get people to tune in and return on a regular basis. These contests are great ways of moving people off one station and onto your station. The difference here is you're not limited to a set time of day nor competing with other casters.

The point is to get your listeners to respond by signing up for the contest. It's just one more way to get buy-in and collect email information so you can stay in touch with them and market to them.

You Tube

Leveraging You Tube is a powerful way to increase your audience. You Tube owns Google and as such it likes it when a platform has their content uploaded to You Tube. You Tube is connected directly to Google Ranking thus when you place your content onto YouTube with a link to your podcast and associated website it will raise your rankings. If you are lucky enough to garner a lot of views/listens that last for 5 to 60 minutes your ranking will go up even higher.

Another reason for having a set show clock of 30 or 60 minutes as I shared earlier is because it simplifies how you edit and upload your content to You Tube.

Build Bridges with Other Podcasters in Your Niche

Many of today's video and podcast participants who sell their services through these media outlets have tapped into the power of affiliate marketing where each host agrees to promote each others platforms on their own platforms.

When one show host interviews a well know podcaster or marketer they get the permission of that person to send out a twitter, Facebook post or email to their followers stating that they have been interviewed by so and so and to check them out. The audience of that person whom you interview then heads over to your podcast and listens to interview of their favorite marketer (your guest) and is exposed to you.

Many of the current crop of online marketers have huge mailing lists that they either trade or sell to each other which lets each of them promote each others shows/products to their respective mailing lists.

There are many other ways to promote your show. Keep in mind you are online so the more online marketing the better, since people who listen to you are online you need to make it easy to find you online.

Leverage Email Lists

A proven method of growing your email list is by renting the email list of other marketers or like minded individuals. Direct Sales companies have been purchasing quality mail lists from companies or individuals for decades. This way you can reach a new audience with email blast advertising. Since your show is free, people will be more likely to open the email blast and actually come to your site. This is especially true if the featured content is something they will enjoy listening to.

A twist on this is Affiliate Marketing where numerous online marketers who have mailing lists cut deals with marketers who are selling various information based products. These affiliate marketers will send out emails to all their recipients with an active link to said marketers materials. The recipients who open up the email and purchase the product is now exposed to the marketers products. If they buy the product the email list owner gets a percentage of the sale.

This also works for you as a podcaster where you can connect with affiliate marketers and work a deal to have them send out an email blast promoting you to their list. (This will cost you something). Maybe you can swing a deal and interview them on your show (if it makes sense) in return they will send out an email blast advertising t their followers that they can hear the interview they did with you.

Sage Advise from a Twenty Year Podcast Veteran

Leo Laporte a 20 year veteran of podcasting who produces 12 different podcast/radio shows with a combined listenership of 5 million listens per month (Keep in mind that's all 12 shows and he's been doing it for 20 years). Stated the following tips to growing an audience to would be podcasters:

- Build a community
- Don't chase an audience instead find your voice
- Talk about what you love

Taking a Deeper Look at Leo's Advice

First off, I agree with what Leo says but if these tactics sound familiar to you, they are. Every article on blogging and book writing state the exact same thing. The idea of creating community around your platform is preached by every marketing person in existence. That being said, let's take a closer look at what this means to you as a podcaster.

The term community as defined by Leo can also be described in one of the following terms:

- Mavens - Malcolm Gladwell in his book Tipping Point.
- Tribe - Seth Godin in his various books
- Fans - Sports Franchises to Rock Groups live or die by their fan base.
- Followers – Political parties to religious groups all have followers.
- Customers – Businesses survive on repeat purchases by loyal customers.

How do you build a community? There is no short term approach to building a community instead it takes years possibly decades to create a base of loyal followers. Seth Godin (cited above) published his first book back in the mid 90's and now he is a highly sought after speaker, that's nearly 20 years of publishing books and using blogging to get his name in front of the business world.

Your community begins with friends and current clients then expands out from there. So be willing to stay at it for years to grow your audience.

Finding Your Voice

Finding your voice can also be defined as discovering your differences or figuring out what sets you apart from everyone else.

I simply call it your Unique Selling Proposition which we already dealt with in greater detail earlier in this book. It's your USP that will help you create a loyal following.

Talk About What You Love

If you love something it will come across to your audience. If you're just doing time, it also shows. People can detect a phony, they can tell when you aren't sincere, so be sincere. The way you can be sincere is talking about something you are passionate about and have a lot of hands on experience with.

Every well known author, artist and musician create what comes from their heart. They hone what is on the inside in order to create something unique to themselves that forever ties them to their creations. To be sure, all artists borrow from their contemporaries and the greats of the past but they still make what they do their own.

Look at the Tonight Show, each person who has hosted this time slot was their own man and did things that relate to the audience of their time. This is also true with talk show hosts be they broadcast or podcast.

Take a cue from the greats and be yourself. Don't worry about being perfect. It takes time to create a quality show so give yourself some grace and enjoy the process of learning.

13

Harnessing the Power of You Tube

Your Secret Weapon to Gaining Listeners and Rankings

A secret to getting more hits on your website and listens to your podcasts is by re-purposing your podcasts as YouTube broadcasts. It's also an extremely good way to build your brand.

You Tube is a perfect platform to re-broadcast your podcast. Think of YouTube as you would a TV Network. You Tube airs old shows originally aired on mainstream and cable TV along with original content created by independent producers.

Think of You Tube as an online network that carries millions of hours, worth of programming from long lost movies to up to the minute first run made for You Tube shows.

Once you've done well with Podcasting you can also harness You Tube by uploading your shows to it. This will allow you to reach and even larger audience of potential fans. You can even create a dual cast show combining audio/video.

Dual casting is when you record the Video at the same time you record the Podcast or visa versa. This way you are able to offer video footage of you sharing your thoughts via YouTube which is a duplicate of the podcast.

As I said earlier in this book, You Tube is owned by Google so they love to see your website/podcast content connected in some way to You Tube. The more views/listens via You Tube the higher ranking you will get with your website. You must however link your You Tube channel with your website and you must connect your show with You Tube. Using links and directed titles that push people over to your website.

Have you watched a video only to have the host say hey click on my link right here in the corner? They are pushing people to sign up or purchase while they are talking so the video becomes an evergreen marketing tool. Once it's loaded it will continue to reach people for years to come slowly but steadily reaching more and more viewers/listeners to your podcast.

Things to Consider Before Doing You Tube

Added Time

When setting out to use You Tube as an additional platform for your podcast you have to keep in mind doing video is another layer of time both in recording/editing and uploading. An hour long video can take hours to upload unlike podcasts that take a few minutes. Video requires a lot of memory so it takes 10 to 20 times the amount of memory to create and much longer time to upload.

A good way to deal with this is uploading the show just before you leave from work or go to bed at night. That way when you wake up or get back in the office the show will have been uploaded.

The simplest way is to grab your self a video editing software tool something you can download directly to your computer. Once you have it uploaded you will have a slight learning curve. After you learn your way around the software its time to upload the audio (MP3 file) to the video program. After this you will need to upload a visual to go along with the video. I suggest you create simple yet attention grabbing image that includes your logo, head shot and show description.

I build my image(s) using Illustrator then export as a Jpeg file. You can use whatever drawing program you're used to. In order to save time, I create the original background image that is used with all the shows. Every time I need a new image I open up the image add the show description then export it as a Jpeg under the new title.

When making your image, make sure to include your website address in the picture. This way you're always directing people to the home page of your blog/website.

Another tip is to create an intro audio bumper stating this is a rebroadcast of you original podcast and for more info they can visit your website. This should be run at the very beginning of the podcast which you add using your video software.

For more about how to do video production and editing I suggest you contact a video software producer/editor to help you out in this department. Who knows, maybe your child knows how to do this if so you can get them on board to help you. Of course if you're a business you probably can pay someone inside your company or a freelance designer.

Added Cost

The cost of repurposing your podcast is pretty small except for the cost in time. If you plan on doing a video cast of yourself while doing the podcast then the cost of creating a quality video can add up. Yes you can create a poorly lighted non professional video as in "here I am talking to you in front of my laptop camera" type of video. Keep in mind these types of video are used all the time for quick announcements.

If you're going to do a video I suggest you purchase some professional quality lighting and a good camera. Of course you could begin with a well lit office space and a cell phone camera on a makeshift tripod. You can also go all out and buy a real tripod and a professional camera and full lighting system and hire someone to video tape you while you're doing the podcast. You may opt for doing a live feed using the Facebook Live service now being offered through Facebook. This way you can take tweets from listeners during the show to ask questions of the guest or hosts.

My feeling is the more professional looking your video the classier you will look to viewers and prospective sponsors who will be attracted to your video.

TV shows have become masters of re-broadcasting their content via You Tube within a day of the airing or even sooner. A perfect example is the Jimmy Fallon show. You can often see a snippet of his show being aired on YouTube the day after the network airs it. This does a lot to keep the buzz building and will work to drive people to watch the show itself. In these cases the network is paying a staff person to repurpose the show and is paying for these shows to end up on the front page of You Tube.

Keep in mind the creation of a You Tube Video is quite long and the uploading time is even longer so you may wish to hold off using You Tube until you get the podcasting down pat.

14

Some Hard Questions

Now that you have gone through all the ins and outs of podcasting I want to ask you a series of questions designed to help you decide if creating a podcast is for you or not.

Why Do You Really Want to Podcast?

Have you always harbored the dream of one day being a Radio Show Host and Podcasting is a low cost way to follow your dream? That's why I went into podcasting.

I have long been a huge fan of radio broadcasting since I was a child I began listening to top 40 songs on my Tube Powered AM Radio my dad gave me as a pre-teen. As a teen I would enjoy listing to radio specials on the FM station which highlighted a band. I also enjoyed and recorded many a Sunday night King Biscuit Hour featuring rock bands of the 70's.

When I began my first professional career in 1980 I was given my own cubicle to work in. To give my mind something to think about while I worked I discovered and fell in love with talk radio.

My love for radio led me to rent air time on a local radio station in 2006 where I hosted a 2 hour late night rock show. My love for radio led me to partner with a 24/7 Streaming Rock Station for 2 years. It also led me into podcasting in 2007 when I launched The Hog Radio Show.

My love for podcasting and broadcasting has brought me to writing this book. It has also led me to offer my expertise to both individuals and corporations to help them launch a successful and even profitable podcast platform that will help them grow their customer base and earn them high props by their peers.

Maybe you are just like me and that's why you want to explore the world of Podcasting. Hopefully this book has given you the insights you need to make the most and spend the least in order to create and produce a professional podcast.

Are You Looking for Out of the Box Ways to Market Yourself?

Podcasting is indeed a profitable platform to leverage on behalf of your company as an extension of your overall marketing efforts. Podcasting can be an inexpensive way to test the waters should you wish to eventually rent airtime and place your show into national syndication through the traditional radio station route. It is a perfect media vehicle to expand your brand and build credibility amongst your customer base. For retailers it allows also you another means of creating co-op advertising partnerships with your suppliers.

Are you Looking for Ways to Expand Your Media Platform?

Podcasting is a perfect platform for any media entity looking to expand its brand without sinking a lot of money into doing so. It is a perfect extension of what you are already doing be it a blog, website, magazine, TV show or You Tube show. As a media company you are always looking at ways to:

- Grow your sponsor base
- Generate more ad revenue
- Increase subscribers

- Elevate your platform
- Increase opportunities to reach more people on behalf of your current sponsors
- To open doors for Joint Ventures with non-competing entities

Podcasting is a perfect vehicle for doing this.

What Will You Be Covering on Your Show?

I have asked this question before but it bears repeating. What type of format do you envision having? What do you want to cover?

Do You Have the Resources to Produce a Quality Podcast?

It's never a good idea to go off half-cocked. You need to make a list of things you'll need to accomplish in order to produce your podcast. Once you have that list checked off you're now ready to begin creating your show.

When I got the idea of producing a podcast about motorcycling I made a list of what I needed to do to make it happen. This list included:

- Locating/contacting people who were doing podcasting
- Finding a host
- Purchasing equipment
- Learning how to use equipment
- Finding guests
- Much more

Fortunately for you, the book you are reading contains all you need to know, with the exception of learning how to use your Audio Software and recording equipment, to begin producing a professional podcast.

By the way, I found my co-host by calling a local motorcycle dealership and meeting with their marketing person who gave me the name of Walt. I followed his advice contacted Walt and 9 years later Walt and I are still working together.

Do You Have Enough Expertise to Bring to The Table?

Everyone has an opinion but opinions are just that, opinions. Keep in mind the reason why people listen to podcasts is the same reason they watch TV or listen to the radio. They wish to be entertained, informed, inspired and learn something new. The personalities who do well in Media are people who can do all of these things within their shows.

The best in the biz either know something they can talk about for hours. This can be fishing, racing, sports, music or TV shows. The point is this; it's a very good idea that you have enough knowledge to share something worth while otherwise you will run out of energy and become boring.

The best way to overcome your lack of knowledge is through the interview format. This is what we do with The Hog Radio Show. We bring on guests and I have a list of questions we run through with our guests. The guest answers a few easy questions and as they get comfortable they begin sharing stories and the show takes on a life of its own.

Questions should not be hard and fast but triggers used to get things rolling in a specific direction. I always have twice as many questions put together than is needed. If you are a curious person, that is a very good place to be. Curiosity mated with a list of quality questions paired with a genuine interest in the guest will allow you to create powerful podcast.

Let's face it none of the Late Night Talk Shows on TV are very knowledgeable people (related to the topics or people they interview) instead they rely on a list of questions. They are good in front of a TV camera and can make you laugh. They are also able to relate to the audience which goes a long way in TV.

The audio world is different as you need much more interaction with guest or being by yourself since the audience can't see anything.

The point is this: You don't have to be Jimmy Fallen or a Rush Limbaugh to do a talk show you just have to be well prepared and have a willingness to ask lots of good questions.

What Sets you Apart from Everyone Else?

It's what makes you different from everyone else that will help establish you as a thought leader, or a podcaster, people will want to listen to. That's why I have included a section in this book about discovering your USP. Your USP is the honest portrayal of yourself that comes through the mic that will endear you to people. Remember, this is not acting, it's being real and if you're not comfortable with being real then maybe podcasting isn't for you.

Do You Have the Time to Podcast?

Have you figured out the actual amount of time it will take to do your podcast? If done right it will take a few hours a week. But when you include creating your outline, booking guests, editing, marketing and uploading you'll have several hours invested. A good rule of thumb is: For every hour of on air time you'll spend 6 to 10 hours a week of off air time.

For those who understand the power of social media you will be light years ahead of those who don't. Social media from Tweeting to Facebooking can grow your audience quicker than those who aren't as up to speed in these arenas.

Bottom line the better you become the less hours you will invest.. Unless your are creating a in-depth history show which includes huge amounts of research time you'll be fine.

Do You Have a Support Network?

It's always a good idea to have the backing of family members who will be affected by the amount of time and money you spend doing podcasting. It's a good idea to have the support of your spouse (if your married) otherwise you may begin hearing things like: "When are you going to make money from this?" "When will you stop spending so much time on your hobby?" These questions will arise from time to time so be prepared for them when they come.

I used to play music in rock bands for a 10 year period of my life. When I got married my wife already knew this and she supported it. I quit doing this and eventually decided I wanted to do a radio show. She supported me on this even though I had to take a loan out in order to rent air time.

After not getting sponsors onboard, I had to stop doing the show. She was disappointed I couldn't make a go of it but she supported me none the less. When I went into podcasting she again supported me knowing I need some type of creative outlet.

Note: I don't have other extra curricular activities that I indulge in, such as hunting, fishing or golfing all of which take up lots of time and money. The point is this; unless you have support it will become a chore not a positive experience.

Are You Willing to Not Make Money From It?

As I said before most people never make any money at podcasting no matter how many podcast courses state otherwise. Most do it because they are passionate and wish to use podcasting as their creative outlet. Yes the Companies and Media platforms who go into it can make money from it because its part of their marketing/business plan. But for most individuals you need to approach podcasting as a hobby with possible long range small monetary returns.

Do You Have a Product or Service You Wish to Promote?

For those of you who are looking into podcasting as a means of raising awareness of your services and products I can't think of a better way to do so. The cost to return is very good. From my point of view podcasting is a very effective tool for consultants, coaches, service providers and information based product marketers. It's a wonderful way to get the word out about your services or products in a non selling manner. Podcasting is a powerful way to elevate your self above your peers and competitors. Having a show gives you cache, much like authoring a book does.

Is This a Short Term or Long Term Endeavor?

It might be a good idea to give yourself a time limit to see if what you are doing is an effective enough use of your time. Once you have set up a time frame you can verify return on effort and move forward to make adjustments and possibly slip out of podcasting or switch to a different format if things don't pan out as expected.

Keep in mind it takes time to build an audience especially if you are starting out with little to no connections to promote to. The bigger your contact list the faster you can grow your show.

By creating an exit plan ahead of time you are giving yourself a way out should things not go your way. It will prevent you from getting so immersed you can't let go when you should quit.

Failure is just another word for experience. No one is a failure who tries something and doesn't get the result they hoped for. So don't get discouraged if after investing time and money you don't end up where you hoped to be. Take the experience and cherish it and celebrate the fact you did something others would never try to do.

Is There a Market or Interest in What You Have to Offer?

This is always a good question you should ask yourself before any business venture. Too many companies never proved the interest level beyond family and friends to ferret out if it was a good idea and end up losing their shirt. The same thing can be said of radio shows and podcasts. Is there any interest in what you are sharing? Are there Magazines, blogs, TV shows devoted to the topic you will be covering? If yes then that's a very good sign, if not, then it might be a bad omen and you should steer clear and not do it.

Ask yourself, has anyone done what you wish to do? If they have, how successful are they and can you learn from them.

15

So You Want to Be a Talk Star

In the world of podcasting and broadcasting there are a handful of talk stars that have been able to take their format and grow it into various other ventures.

Some talk shows started on Radio and then added TV while others started in TV and went to radio then back to TV (Bill ORiliey). There are those who started locally on a single station and then got themselves syndicated and are now heard on hundreds of stations. There are also the podcasters who started out doing radio and went 100% to the podcast format. There are those who started in podcasting and never left or have expanded into other ventures.

In this chapter we will examine who should think about doing a podcast from a monetary point of view and what the real numbers look like in podcasting and why so many advertisers are hesitant to air ads on your podcast.

A long time service provider in the podcast arena shared some startling facts related to podcasting I think bears looking at.

Know Your Numbers

Unless you use a tracking service attached to your podcast feed you have no way of knowing how many listens/downloads you have. Without numbers you have no way to know who is listening to your podcast(s). To remedy this, I suggest you make sure to choose a tracking service/provider who offers it and pay the small yearly fee to have your show tracked.

Two services that offer tracking are: Blubrry Powercast and PODOMATIC. Both platforms allow you to get your podcast listed in iTunes and other well-known platforms which is what you need to have in place in order to reach the masses.

In the world of podcasting you have to be especially careful when reading your statistics as they can often be deceiving. The following are things that need to be tracked.

1. The number of overall plays/downloads (listens)
2. The number of plays/downloads (listens) per episode*

*This number is the most important number as it shows exactly how many people are listening to each show whereas the other number reflects a collective number. For simplicity sake let me show you what I am talking about. (Please note; I will lump downloads and listens under the titles downloads and episode).

The number of actual listeners you have.

- 100 listeners download Episode One which equates to 100 listens per Episode One for a total of 100 downloads.
- Same 100 listeners download Episode Two which equates to 100 listens per Episode Two for a total of 200 downloads
- Same 100 listeners download Episode Three which equates to 100 listens per Episode Three for a total of 300 downloads
- Same 100 listeners download a total to 10 Episodes which equates 100 listens per Episode for a total of 1000 downloads.

Let's say each week you add 10 new listeners who listen to each new episode but also go back and begin listening to all the old episodes, now you have some pretty wild numbers to work with. So how do you keep track of actual listeners from total downloads?

Just do a per episode statistic report. For simplicity sake lets say that number is 500 downloads per episode for the past 4 weeks. You can assume your audience is close to 500 listeners.

The only time the overall number makes sense is when you are selling advertisers on the number of impressions (downloads) they will get for each ad spot they run during your show. This is how ad agencies sell ad spots.

When you go to talk to advertisers (should you wish to bring any on) 100 listeners is useless to them because they want to reach 40,000 listeners not 100. That said you can still be the biggest fish in your pond.

Bottom line, numbers do count but its how you count those numbers and what those numbers represent that allows you to leverage your show. The smaller the niche the more direct you can be, the larger the niche the more general you will be. Let me explain.

Understanding Your Niche

Most of you have probably heard of a niche market. Do you know what the term means? Let me give you an example. A niche market would be women over 65. If you were going to build a show around this group's needs and interests you would have to do some home work.

What ways do most of these women get their media? Probably they get it through traditional TV and Radio. This being the case, starting a podcast for women over 65 would probably not get many listeners. You would do far better to create a radio show and air it on your local Public Radio Station that caters to this demographic.

Who would you go after for advertisers? Again what do women 65 and older purchase a lot of? You'll have to do your homework again. Once you have that dialed in you could seek out sponsors whose products meet these women's needs and interest.

Lets say you decide this group loves to travel be it tour busses, cruses and European tours. Then why not create a travel show and air it on a station that gets lots of listeners or viewers from within this demographic.

Guess what? That's what Rick Steves has done. He uses the Public Airwaves to broadcast his travel shows TV shows both radio and TV. Since he is promoting himself and his tours he doesn't need to "sell" you anything or rely on sponsors. Instead he is one big infomercial.

Rick is the master of the infomercial programming. No one comes close to what he does. He knows his demographic and works very hard to promote himself using media platforms that cater to them.

The point is this, know who you wish to reach and make sure your audience listens to podcasts.

Who Should Think About Podcasting?

From a purely business standpoint the following service providers will benefit most by having a weekly podcast.

- Personal Coaches
- Consultants
- Service providers (Dave Ramsey)
- Christian Ministries
- Media Entities
- Specialty Retailers (Cabela's)
- Organizations
- Linked In groups
- Network Marketing Companies
- Business Networking Groups
- Trade Associations
- Anyone with a large email base
- Experience based Retailers
- Niche Industries
- Authors/Speakers/Self Help

- Health and Wellness Providers

These are but a few examples of who could benefit from having a podcast. The point is this, by having a purpose and a plan in place you will be in the best position to leverage your show to best serve your customer base.

Not everyone should go into podcasting but for those who have a plan, the right information and an ongoing marketing campaign in place you can truly benefit from this unique and growing media platform.

A Few Examples

A podcast is a perfect way to elevate your self and build trust and market yourself to current and potential customers.

Let's say you're a business coach and all you want is 40 clients at any given time then creating a podcast that reaches 100 people per week is worth while because out of this 100 you may very well get 5 clients. Let's say you reach 1,000 people on a regular basis again your odds of landing 5 to 10 clients is very good.

Podcasting is your means of building trust amongst a very small but select group of potential clients. A perfect example of this is a local law practice that has a radio show on a local station. He has a call in show and where he offers advice along with directing people to his free seminars which typically sell out. Out of those seminars he will net a handful of clients who will pay well for his services. He will also get phone calls, emails to his practice throughout the week from listeners who have been listening to his show. He can afford the $1,500.00 a month it costs him to rent air time on this station because he will generate 10 times that investment of time and money, if he didn't he would be off the air. As it is he has been on this station for quite some time.

Let's say you have a wellness clinic, you can choose to go onto a local radio station and rent airtime for $250.00 to $500.00 per hour each week. You will draw attention to yourself and gain trust in the eyes of those who listen to your show and probably funnel people to your clinic or free seminar. But let's say you did the same show via podcast and you leveraged all your social media and email list and sent invites to all your current clients and invited them to listen and share you with all their friends.

You can post the podcast on your website and in all electronic literature, Linked In connections and your Facebook connections. Guess what? You will probably come up with a list of several hundred people who will likely tune you in and one by one, they will share you with their friends and thus you grow your audience.

By growing yourself online verses a radio show it may take several months to reach the same number of people you would by airing your show on a local radio station but the savings is well worth it.

So there is power on podcasting especially if you have a very refined tight demographic you wish to reach, not the entire world.

16
That's all Folks!

Back in my childhood I would eagerly await Saturday mornings so I could get up grab my blanket and sit in front of the TV for a few hours watching my favorite cartoons. At the end of the block of cartoons came the Warner Brothers Cartoon Hour later renamed The Looney Tunes Hour. After nearly an hour of watching all the skits featuring everyone from Bugs Bunny to Wiley Coyote the show would come to an end. The end was when all the characters would come onto the stage singing a little tune called *On With The Show Let us Go*. At the end of this song and dance number the characters would dance off the stage and the curtain would fall. Once the curtain fell a little hole would appear and grow in size and then out would pop one of the characters usually Bugs Bunny or Porky Pig. When Porky's head would pop out of the curtain he would say "Tha, tha, tha, that's all folks" and the show would be over.

As child I knew my time in front of the TV was over and it was on to my chores. So when the song came on it would evoke a bit of sadness. It meant I had to wait another week before I could watch my favorite cartoon characters.

This chapter is my farewell to you, but just like the shows ending, it's not really over. There is something to look forward to, such as doing one of the following things:

- Re-reading this book and applying it to the creation of your podcast.

- Deciding now is not a good time to start podcasting.
- Contacting me directly, to seek my advice or help in producing a podcast.

Whatever you decide I want to let you know I am here to help you out should you have need. I would also love to hear from you about your adventures in podcasting as well as get your feed-back on what you thought about my book and if there is something I should include in the next edition should I choose to do a second edition. You can contact me through my website stevejohann.com.

But before I say *That's All Folks,* I would like to leave you with a few parting thoughts.

My Entry into the World of Podcasting

Back in 2006 I chased my dream of becoming a radio show host. I decided to mate my love of music with my love for talk radio and began looking into what it would take to go on the radio and host my own show. After much research I decided I could rent time from a local station for the cost of $125.00 per hour for two hours on Saturday nights. My times were 10PM to 12AM.

That show was called the Sacred Rock Radio Show featuring 4 decades of Christian Rock Music. I got a private loan for $5,000.00 and I gathered all my friends CD's together with my own and started putting together a 2 hour block of music and commentary between songs. I went on the air late spring of 2006 and began airing my show.

During this time I also set up my lap top with the ability to stream the show while I was broadcasting live. This is what introduced me to the world of streaming and online media. I also paid someone to build a Sacred Rock Radio website to support the show.

I then began chasing after would be sponsors but found it difficult to get anyone on board. On average I invested nearly 8 hours a week pre-production to get ready for the 2 hour show I did on air. I created a show clock so I could make sure all the songs fit within the time period between commercial breaks and still allow me time to share my thoughts about the artists and music I was featuring.

I loved hosting a show on the radio but I also was fast running out of money and still had no sponsors after several weeks of being on air. I was at a crossroads and I needed guidance. I thought through who I knew in the radio industry I could contact who might be able to advise me. I remembered a person I had met briefly who fit this description.

I called him up and asked him if he could meet with me to go over what I should do. He said yes, that would be no problem but it would cost me $400.00 to meet with him for an hour. I said thanks but I had run out of money and couldn't afford his time. So I hung up.

I don't know if it was the same day of the next but it wasn't very long and he called back and said to me "Hey Steve you know what, for the price of a cup of coffee I will meet with you for 30 minutes". We set up the appointment and we met the following week.

After that 30 minute conversation I was much the wiser and I knew I had to sever my ties with the station. I immediately called the radio station and said I would be canceling my show with them. This left me four more weeks of shows to fulfill my contract obligations.

To say I was disappointed would be an understatement. The only thing I had to show for my time and money was 3 months, worth of shows saved on CD's. Well that's not all I also left with a couple of peoples names I didn't have before I went into the radio business. Both helped me move into the wonderful world of podcasting.

Shortly after leaving the radio world, I partnered with the owner of a 24/7 Online Streaming Radio Station called Tri Rock where, for the next 2 years, I worked to find advertisers and place our feed onto radio stations. During my time with Tri Rock I built up an arsenal of connections and learned a lot about the world of Broadcasting and online streaming.

It was during this time we needed to find a way to bring in revenue without selling ad space around the music programming. I began to explore various show formats. To make a long story short, I came up with a show about Motorcycling which I named the Hog Radio Show.

I went and purchased the equipment I needed to build my own home studio. After learning the equipment, I called the host and we started our first show together in the third room of my house which doubled as my home office at the time.

Over the years I've had the show aired on several traditional radio stations and online networks only to see the stations change formats or the networks go under. This has not kept me from growing the audience through some of the very methods outlined in this book.

The point of my story is to give you a brief insight into what I have had to go through. Radio and podcasting is not easy but well worth the effort and time. Podcasting is an excellent vehicle to build your brand and promote yourself. It's also s a fun way to share your thoughts and meet some very cool people.

Being on the air is a pretty potent thing.

Conclusion

Consider this book your opportunity to buy me a few cups of coffee where I divulge my knowledge with you. Possibly you have already begun to question your need to create a podcast at this time. That's a good place to be. Possibly you're ready to move forward. That's an exciting place to be.

Podcasting isn't for everyone but it may be just right for you. Should you wish to seek my advice or help in creating a podcast for your company you can contact me through my email steve@stevejohann.com.

Just as You Tube has made stars out of upstarts with the willingness to be original and work hard, podcasting also provides you the very same opportunity. So why not chase your dream and start podcasting!

Quick update. When I first wrote this book, I was using Adobe Audition. Just as I was ready to publish this book my computer that held my Audio Software died. After purchasing a new computer, I needed to find a replacement for my old Adobe product. After much research, I ended up purchasing **Acustica's Mixcraft 8** *which includes a built in MP3 exporting capability and is very similar in the way it works to what I have been used to using.*

Here's to your success.

Steve Johann
Producer, Creator and Communicator
steve@stevejohann.com
www.stevejohann.com

www.ingramcontent.com/pod-product-compliance
Lightning Source LLC
Chambersburg PA
CBHW021408170526
45164CB00002B/551